More Praise for
Creative Community Organizing

"Make room, Howard Zinn! Si Kahn's *Creative Community Organizing* deserves a place on the must-read shelf next to *A People's History of the United States*. Warm, cheerful, candid, and wise—just like the man himself—Si's book is more than a how-to for justice seekers, more than a gripping memoir from the front lines of bodacious modern activism. It's the up-close and creative story of how the 'people's history' gets made."

—Jay Harris, Publisher, *Mother Jones*

"Si Kahn's latest book is a great addition to strategic community organizing, offering nuanced insights into the difficult and often life-saving fights organizers wage on a daily basis for social justice, human rights, and progressive change."

—Rinku Sen, President and Executive Director, Applied Research Center; Publisher, *ColorLines*; and coauthor of *The Accidental American*

"*Creative Community Organizing* reminds us of the power of music and storytelling for deep transformation. Magic happens when we bring together creativity with strategy. Si gives us the recipe for moving to a future where human rights for all can become possible."

—Mallika Dutt, Executive Director, Breakthrough

"Si Kahn is a Renaissance man for the social movements of our generation. He is a troubadour, a poet, and a lyricist; a thoughtful and reflective writer; a committed organizer and institution builder; and a carrier of his family's and his faith's deepest values. Most of all, he is a passionate believer in social justice and the power of ordinary people to stand up and determine their destinies. Reading this beautifully written and uplifting narrative will give faith and hope to all who read it and take it to heart."

—Miles Rapoport, President, Demos

"*Creative Community Organizing* documents Si Kahn's career of working for justice in ways that are deeply affecting, personally and culturally. Si is truly Democracy's Troubadour, bringing us not just the songs and stories of democracy and justice but also the practical strategies to deepen our democratic roots."

—Congresswoman Tammy Baldwin

"Si Kahn is an organizer and an activist. He's also a poet, a songwriter, a preservationist, a historian, a documentarian in song. He's a stark realist and simultaneously an unflinching optimist. The tender reverence he holds for the people whose struggles he has facilitated spills over into his writing, keeping their stories alive, connecting us to them—and ultimately, ourselves."

—Kathy Mattea, Grammy-winning singer

"Over a lifetime of social justice activism—much of it spent on the front lines—Si has kept the faith with courage, creativity, and humor. His bedrock belief in the power of people working together to create a just world is the spirit that guides this remarkable book."

—Alan Jenkins, Executive Director, The Opportunity Agenda

"The true moxie of *Creative Community Organizing* comes from Si Kahn's brilliant storytelling and his own distinguished career as an organizer, folksinger, and all-around rabble-rouser—exemplifying all that is great about fighting for justice and working for progressive social change. This book is a great primer for organizers, activists, and those dedicated to movement building."

—Pronita Gupta, Director of Programs, Women Donors Network

"Si Kahn has been my mentor, song leader, and conscience since I started organizing two decades ago. From his strategic wisdom, I've learned about organizing smart campaigns, about winning and losing and never giving up. From his songs and stories, I've been connected to the beauty and pain and shared vision that make it possible to keep on fighting. Si combines the brass tacks of organizing with the soulful, collective, creative yearning for the world-as-it-should-be."

—Brad Lander, New York City Councilmember,
39th District (Brooklyn)

"In this marvelous book, Si Kahn leads us through his own history as an organizer for progressive social change and in the process provides an education for future generations to get involved in bringing justice to more of the world's people. His insights on the importance of integrating artistic expression into strategies for change are invaluable."

—John Stocks, Deputy Executive Director,
National Education Association

"Classic recipe: Mix classic storytelling with 2 cups autobiography, 3/4 cup textured folk/movement/gospel poetry set to music, 1/2 cup U.S. history, 2 spoons tested advice, a dash of nostalgia, and a smidgen of medieval history and literature. Blend well with love, encouragement, rejuvenation, faith, and a lifetime of commitment. Get Si Kahn's classic book, *Creative Community Organizing*: a great lesson plan for teaching organizers but also a must-read for anyone who cares about progress and how to make it happen."

—Congressman Mel Watt

"Si Kahn has the heart of a poet, the wit of a comedian, the hands of a seasoned political operative, and the ability to explain to the rest of us how to translate dreams into day-to-day reality. This is one of the most illuminating and personal books ever written by a real-life progressive hero."

—Danny Goldberg, author of *Bumping into Geniuses*

"There is so much hope in Si Kahn's new book: it is filled with stories spanning four decades of his creativity tackling some of our country's toughest problems. He may not have invented the term 'creative community organizing,' but he has certainly shaped its past and future."

—Geraldine Laybourne, founder, Oxygen Media

"In *Creative Community Organizing*, Si distills forty-five years of experience for another generation that is already picking up the fight for a just and democratic future. Poet, songwriter, and storyteller par excellence, he weaves memoir and organizing manual into a unique and inspiring tapestry. This book is a gift to the rest of us, a challenge never to lose faith in human possibility or to back off from doing the work of joining with others to build a better world."

—Sara M. Evans, author of *Born for Liberty*

"My union brother Si Kahn and I have been friends for over thirty years. His first book, *How People Get Power*, was my introduction to organizing and my initial inspiration for what has been a wonderful life working to build collective action and to struggle together for the common good. What better hope for *Creative Community Organizing* than that it will help create that dynamic in the lives of others."

—Stewart Acuff, Assistant to the President, AFL-CIO

"Si Kahn's compelling portraits remind us that creative community organizing is all about people—real-life individuals who use their skills to take on enormous challenges and those whose lives are made better as a result. This is an inspiring and instructive read."

—Congresswoman Jan Schakowsky

"Si writes with a calm passion. This book is a kind, caring friend and mentor for we who are engaged in the struggle to help our country live up to the promise of what America was meant to be."

—Ben Cohen, cofounder, Ben & Jerry's Homemade Ice Cream

"Si Kahn's powerful, stirring story of his lifelong journey for justice and lessons learned will captivate and energize all who care about equal justice. This is *the* handbook for rabble-rousers everywhere!

—Ada Deer, Distinguished Lecturer Emerita, School of Social Work and
American Indian Studies Program, University of Wisconsin–Madison;
former Assistant Secretary of Indian Affairs; and past chair, Menominee Tribe

"In his forty-five years as a labor, civil rights, and community organizer, Si Kahn has maintained his unshakeable faith in the capacity of working people to shape their own destiny and his passionate belief that what this country needs more than anything else is a strong progressive labor movement. His work and his songs are a testimony to the power of the union."

—John McCutcheon, President, Local 1000,
American Federation of Musicians, AFL-CIO

"Organizing is not simply a toolbox of strategies, charts, and tactics. Organizing for social and economic justice demands deep relationships, core unshakeable values, humility born of experience, and appreciation of the creative spirit in all of us. Si Kahn, a marathon runner for justice, crams a lifetime of experience and wisdom into this highly readable and inspirational book—a must-read for anyone in the trenches or thinking about joining the struggle for justice."

—Kim Bobo, Executive Director, Interfaith Worker Justice

"Si Kahn's unique combination of folk songs and prose provides a riveting memoir and analysis of class struggle as well as an inspirational organizing tool. This book will become a cornerstone of the movement for social justice."

—Stephen Nathan, editor, *Prison Privatisation
Report International*, London, England

"Reading a Si Kahn book is like listening to his music—organizing stories come alive and we learn while listening and imagining. This is an equally great read for community and workplace organizers."
—Larry Cohen, President, Communications
Workers of America

"Si Kahn, the grandchild of immigrants, is a gifted storyteller who conveys the story of community organizing in a way it's never been told. His account of the campaign to abolish so-called immigrant family detention leaves the reader with hope and inspiration."
—Daranee Petsod, Executive Director, Grantmakers
Concerned with Immigrants and Refugees

"*Creative Community Organizing* provides the reader with an opportunity to listen to and learn from one of the field's legendary practitioners. As someone who has benefited firsthand from Si's insight and inspiration, first as an organizer and more recently as the CEO of the Jewish Funds for Justice—the foundation Si helped create to fund community organizing—I commend this book to anyone seeking to understand what organizing at its best can look like."
—Simon Greer, President and CEO, Jewish Funds for Justice

"Si, master organizer, storyteller, and musician, uses his poetic, lyrical prose to teach and inspire. This is a book you'll read in one sitting and remember the lessons because the stories will stay with you forever."
—Jackie Kendall, Executive Director, Midwest Academy

"Si Kahn beautifully weaves poetry, song, stories, remembrances, analysis, and prescriptions into a rich tapestry. He transports the reader through forty-five years of community and labor organizing, from roots with the Student Nonviolent Coordinating Committee in 1965 through recent decades as founder and executive director of Grassroots Leadership. This is a deeply personal book, firmly planted in his religious Jewish upbringing by his father, a very musical rabbi, and his mother, who taught him the love of poetry. Read this book to learn from a consummate organizer, educator, and cultural worker."
—Neil Tudiver, Assistant Executive Director,
Canadian Association of University Teachers

"If 'the arc of the moral universe bends toward justice,' as Martin Luther King said, then Si Kahn has devoted his life to riding that arc. His powerful impulse to service, combined with deep compassion, is a force of nature. I put Si in the same category as Woody Guthrie, as Pete Seeger, and in a strange way, as my dad, who shared his righteous sense of humanity and his love of the 'meek,' who he truly believed would 'inherit the earth.'"

—Rosanne Cash, writer and musician

"When we start singing again, we'll start winning again. Si Kahn is the bridge between organizing and singing for social justice, and his new book is an inspiration."

—Robert Kuttner, coeditor, *The American Prospect*

"Those who know Si Kahn's work will want to sign on and march once again with this uniquely moving and cheerful leader! Si's new book, embellished with many of his lyrics, is touching, personal, and stirring, filled with practical advice and analysis about organizing that can be found nowhere else. Si will convince you that you can change the world and that you should."

—Tim Coulter, attorney; founder, National Indian Law Resource Center; and member, Citizen Potawatomi Nation

"This beautifully written book captures the connections of Jewish values and American democratic ideals as memorably, movingly, and vividly as any I have read. An inspiring, remarkably insightful, and urgently needed treasure for social justice activists everywhere."

—Rabbi David Saperstein, Director, Religious Action Center of Reform Judaism

"This book is the perfect road map for activists and the average citizen, a testament to the power of the human spirit, and a fantastic journey through history with a tour guide who regularly exhibits compassion, accountability, and integrity."

—Melissa Bradley, Senior Strategist, Green for All

"Si Kahn's stories and songs tell us about him and about ourselves. Like all great songs, these stay in your head and in your heart. Si tells about his own roots and the wins, near wins, and nowhere at all near wins—and we learn to look into our own roots, our own wins, our own stories for sustenance and wisdom."

—David Beckwith, Executive Director, The Needmor Fund

"Si Kahn draws on his multiple gifts as an organizer, historian, songwriter, and storyteller to give us a new book that makes a compelling case for the integration of cultural work into traditional community organizing. Grassroots Leadership's campaign to end immigrant family detention, which is part of larger struggles against for-profit prisons and for equal justice, shows again the powerful impact of culture, self-knowledge, and knowledge of other people's histories. This campaign has ignited a movement of allies centered on those directly affected by the policy but reaching far beyond. This is organizing that will outlast any one campaign."

—Taryn Higashi, Executive Director,
Unbound Philanthropy

"Si does a superb job in this book, as he does in life, of bringing the songs and stories of the movement into his organizing. This book speaks so well to the culture of organizing that Si has developed around him and that I have learned so much about through him."

—Jacob Flowers, Executive Director,
Mid-South Peace and Justice Center

"Si Kahn, a gifted grassroots organizer, welcomes us to his lifelong struggle for justice, telling us how culture can help people who are marginalized, disenfranchised, and dispossessed build power to achieve equity and justice for all. The book is a powerful guide to action and to achieving transformative change. It is great reading whether you are a potential organizer or just a regular Jo/Joe. Get your beverage and sit down for a great journey."

—Joanie Bronfman, sociologist, musician, and activist

"Si Kahn's book is chock-full of compelling stories drawn from his four decades of experience as an organizer in many of the most important social movements of our time. The book itself is powerful evidence for one of Si's themes—that telling stories is the most powerful means of communicating the culture and values that lie at the core of the movement for social and economic justice. You'll love this book if you are an experienced organizer or if you've begun to wonder if you should stop just studying history and start making it."

—Robert Creamer, organizer, strategist, and
political consultant and author of
Stand Up Straight

"Si Kahn's guide to creative community organizing is an extraordinary tour de force, as only he could write it—passionate and intensive, wise and comedic. It is a brilliant and moving mixture of autobiography, song, American history, and vision, striving always toward the future we hope to build."

—Ruth W. Messinger, President, American Jewish World Service

"In *Creative Community Organizing*, Si Kahn reminds us of the transformational capacity of our organizing work and challenges us to engage in a contemplative practice that is capable of making sense of how and why we struggle. His text is a deep and profound narrative of respect for those who, like him, have been compelled to dedicate their lives to the cause of social justice and human dignity, and we are immeasurably enriched by his words."

—Joseph Jordan, Director, The Sonja Haynes Stone Center for Black Culture and History

"Si Kahn is not just an organizer. He's a Jewish organizer, a 'secular rabbi,' as he calls himself, raised and rooted in those areas of Jewish history, tradition, and religion that cry out for democracy and equity. As a Jewish feminist, I hope that whatever faith or secular commitment people may have, they will also find the courage to lift up the parts of their tradition that reach out toward openness and reject any text or teaching that, based on gender or sexual orientation, sees any human being as less than any other."

—Barbara Dobkin, founder and Chair, Ma'yan: The Jewish Women's Project

"CrossCurrents is a new foundation that works at the intersection of art and social justice and instigates collaborations with other funders and artists organizing to strengthen our democracy. In this new book that itself weaves together art and activism, organizer/artist Si Kahn makes a powerful case for culture and cultural work as critical components in any movement for justice."

—Ken Grossinger, Chair, CrossCurrents Foundation

"Restorative for those of us who cut our teeth on movements past, encouraging for those who didn't, moving for all who still believe that we can make justice roll down like water if we do it together and sing."

—Marie C. Wilson, President and founder, The White House Project

"As a union organizer, community organizer, singer/songwriter, and author, Si Kahn has spent his life at the confluence of union and community organizing and art and activism. His books, trainings, and teachings have taught and inspired a generation, and his latest effort, *Creative Community Organizing*, continues this incredible legacy."
—Anna Burger, Chair, Change to Win labor federation,
and Secretary-Treasurer, SEIU

"In this powerful new book, Si Kahn shows us how organizing can help build a society where everyone, including lesbians, gays, bisexuals, and transgendered people, is guaranteed basic equal rights and the full recognition of her and his humanity. It's a vision worth fighting for."
—Harry Knox, Director, Religion and Faith Program,
Human Rights Campaign Foundation

"Out of the richness of Si Kahn's history, woven together with songs he has written, tied with his warmth and decency of human concern, comes this insightful book about how, through organizing, we can build a better world. It can help anyone who cares about justice understand how to make that more likely to become reality. This book moves and inspires."
—Heather Booth, President, Midwest Academy

"Si Kahn and this guide are stuffed with knowledge, advice, and inspiration that are invaluable to anyone organizing for justice."
—James Haslam, Director/Lead Organizer, Vermont Workers' Center,
part of Jobs with Justice and Grassroots Global Justice

"Few people can match Si Kahn's experience of community organizing for social change. This beautifully written book will be a source of much-needed ideas and inspiration for many years to come."
—Michael Edwards, Distinguished Senior Fellow,
Demos, and author of *Small Change*

"There is an ethical dilemma in all journeys for justice. We must struggle with making sure we do not ask of others that which we are unable to give ourselves. Si casts light on the complexities, risks, and rewards of community organizing. In doing so, he elevates the process of social change to the status it deserves, a way of life, with plenty of hills and valleys, not just a 'day job' with a clear beginning and end."
—Selena E. Sermeño, PhD, psychologist, peace and
human rights educator, and dialogue facilitator

"For over thirty years, social workers and social work students have relied on Si Kahn's books as trusted friends and guides. His new book, *Creative Community Organizing*, tells us not only how we can do our community organization work most effectively but why what we do matters so much. It should be on every social worker's desk."

—Barbara White, Dean, School of Social Work, University of Texas at Austin, and past president, National Association of Social Workers and Council on Social Work Education

"The powers that be have so much money they think they can co-opt any one organization. But what are they going to do about the millions of small efforts and organizations going on in communities in every country in the world? Read this book, and learn how you can be part of this great international grassroots movement."

—Pete Seeger, musician

"All those interested in walking even a little way down the road toward change in their own communities or countries will profit from a guide like Si Kahn. Familiar himself with carpentry, auto mechanics, and organizing, Si is not afraid to get his hands dirty. He is a mentor of the highest order who has created a guide to organizing that will allow his experience to benefit us for years to come. This is a legacy-extending book that should reach well into the twenty-first century. I hope it remains in print for one hundred years."

—Scott Ainslie, musician/producer

"A precious gift for our children and their children who dream of making the world a better place, this book weaves memories, stories, songs, political analysis, and histories of struggle into a brilliant, joyful tapestry of organizing and political education that speaks truth to power. This book can haunt and inspire you to action, make you chuckle and laugh out loud!"

—Chandra Talpade Mohanty, author of *Feminism Without Borders*

"You've got to read Si Kahn's *Creative Community Organizing*. It's filled with great stories, empowering lyrics, essential history lessons, and a storehouse of wisdom accumulated from forty-five years of 'pulling his shift,' as he puts it. A joy to read and to share. Pass it on!"

—Matthew Rothschild, Editor, *The Progressive*

CREATIVE COMMUNITY ORGANIZING

CREATIVE COMMUNITY ORGANIZING

A Guide for Rabble-Rousers, Activists, and Quiet Lovers of Justice

SI KAHN

BK

Berrett–Koehler Publishers, Inc.
San Francisco
a BK Currents book

Berrett-Koehler Publishers, Inc.
235 Montgomery Street, Suite 650
San Francisco, CA 94104-2916
Tel: (415) 288-0260   Fax: (415) 362-2512   www.bkconnection.com

Ordering Information
Quantity sales. Special discounts are available on quantity purchases by corporations, associations, and others. For details, contact the "Special Sales Department" at the Berrett-Koehler address above.
Individual sales. Berrett-Koehler publications are available through most bookstores. They can also be ordered directly from Berrett-Koehler: Tel: (800) 929-2929; Fax: (802) 864-7626; www.bkconnection.com
Orders for college textbook/course adoption use. Please contact Berrett-Koehler: Tel: (800) 929-2929; Fax: (802) 864-7626.
Orders by U.S. trade bookstores and wholesalers. Please contact Ingram Publisher Services, Tel: (800) 509-4887; Fax: (800) 838-1149; E-mail: customer.service@ingrampublisherservices.com; or visit www.ingrampublisherservices.com/Ordering for details about electronic ordering.

Berrett-Koehler and the BK logo are registered trademarks of Berrett-Koehler Publishers, Inc.

Printed in the United States of America
Berrett-Koehler books are printed on long-lasting acid-free paper. When it is available, we choose paper that has been manufactured by environmentally responsible processes. These may include using trees grown in sustainable forests, incorporating recycled paper, minimizing chlorine in bleaching, or recycling the energy produced at the paper mill.

Library of Congress Cataloging-in-Publication Data
Kahn, Si.
    Creative community organizing : a guide for rabble-rousers, activists and quiet lovers of justice / Si Kahn.
        p. cm.
    Includes bibliographical references and index.
    ISBN 978-1-60509-444-1 (pbk.)
1. Community organization. 2. Community power. 3. Community activists.
4. Political particpation. I. Title.
    HM776.K35 2009
    307.1'4--dc22
                                        2009042541

First Edition
15 14 13 12 11 10   10 9 8 7 6 5 4 3 2 1

Production: Linda Jupiter Productions   *Copy editor:* Judith Brown
Interior design: Laura Lind Design   *Proofreader:* Henrietta Bensussen
Author photo: Nancy Pierce   *Indexer:* Medea Minnich
Cover design: Ian Shimkoviak, The Book Designers

Once again, for public/feminist philosopher Elizabeth Minnich,
my partner and spouse of more than thirty years, my best friend
for over fifty, who carries on the work of her teacher, Hannah
Arendt, by trying to understand how and why decent people
sometimes agree to participate in sustained group violence; why
they sometimes choose to resist; and how democratic education
can strengthen our ability to say no to collective evil.

CONTENTS

FOREWORD
BY JIM HIGHTOWER

"I guess a small-town mayor is sort of like a community organizer, except that you have actual responsibilities." Thus spoke Governor Sarah Palin in 2008, bless her heart. With that remark, the half-baked Alaskan unintentionally kicked off a national debate about the importance of community organizing.

Palin's too-cute dissing of President Barack Obama's past organizing, which he did in neighborhoods devastated by steel mill closures, prompted community organizers to step out and stand *proud*. (Some T-shirts proclaimed "Jesus was a Community Organizer when Pontius Pilate was a Governor.")

The Obama campaign's grassroots model helped propel him into the presidency, thus sealing the debate over the efficacy of community organizing. I am not suggesting that if you follow Si Kahn's pearls of wisdom *you* will become president. But I can guarantee you that community organizing strengthens our democracy.

And we sure need more and stronger democracy around here. Just about anybody you meet in any Chat & Chew Café in America will tell you that. They know that the barons of Wall Street and the chieftains of global corporations are running everything from America's economic policy to the political system—and running roughshod over working families, family farmers, the middle class, our air and water, and our nation's ethic of the common good. They think they're the top dogs and the rest of us are just a bunch of fire hydrants, which is why Si Kahn's message is so timely and important.

> *Democracy is not something that happens only at election time, and it's not something that happens just with one event. It's an ongoing, grassroots building process.*

What community organizing does is bring people together so they can identify common problems, look for solutions, and craft strategies to reach, educate, and mobilize others, so we can all join together to make the changes we need and deserve.

"One of the greatest skills an organizer can have," Si writes, "is the ability to frame and ask questions in ways that make people not only want to answer them, but also think deeply, and in unexpected ways, about what the answers might be." He isn't talking about sound bites or knee-jerk patriotism or settling for "the way things have always been done around here." Si is talking about creative thinking, about myth-busting and people-first solutions. He is talking about ordinary people making history.

Creative community organizing can transform us into visionaries, prod us to learn new skills, and encourage us to take risks for our and our children's future. Community organizing can change hearts and minds, attitudes, and sometimes even deeply held beliefs. Organizing can tip the balance of power and challenge the old Texas Golden Rule: "Them that has the gold makes the rules."

Technology has given community organizing a huge boost. With just a click of whichever finger you care to use, you can learn about and weigh in on big issues like climate change, war(s), immigration, or for-profit prisons. But high tech cannot replace the need for "high touch"—there is no substitute for people showing up and speaking out at public hearings, PTA meetings, rallies, demonstrations, or picket lines.

Sometimes, just like dancing the Hokey-Pokey, you have to "put your whole self in." *Creative Community Organizing* shows you how people have put their whole selves in and won some amazing victories.

As I read the book, I remembered inspiring moments from the Southern Civil Rights Movement—one of the most creative and significant organizing campaigns in our nation's history. Such moments continue today. For example, Si takes us to the front lines of a new, compelling, and, to some, controversial community organizing effort: the national campaign by Grassroots Leadership to abolish all for-profit private prisons, jails, and detention centers—and to end immigrant family detention (one of the worst ideas the capitalist system has come up with in the last five hundred years). Along the way, he uses incredible stories, humor, songs, culture, philosophy, poetry, history, and unforgettable characters to encourage all of us to become involved in the great challenges of our times.

The best political button I ever saw was one a fellow was wearing at an environmental rally I attended a few years ago in Vermont. It said: "Wearing a Button Is Not Enough." Si's book makes clear that to achieve our ideals of fairness, justice, and equal opportunity for all, we must be more than a nation of button wearers. He shows us that by joining together, grassroots folks really can organize themselves to stand up to the Powers That Be—and produce the democratic change that America needs.

It's my fervent hope that everyone who picks up this book will see the possibilities and join this historic effort.

Jim Hightower
www.jimhightower.com

FOREWORD
BY ANGELA DAVIS

With this book, *Creative Community Organizing: A Guide for Rabble-Rousers, Activists, and Quiet Lovers of Justice*, Si Kahn has achieved an important feat. He has written a memoir, which is also a stirring account of some of the most important contemporary struggles for social justice. He has written a guide to community organizing practices, which is also a collection of inspiring stories that demonstrates how grassroots work can produce striking results. He offers us a written text, which is so thoroughly infused with music that the reader forgets sometimes that she is reading and not listening to (or singing along with) a charismatic song leader—like Pete Seeger, Jane Sapp, or Si Kahn.

As I write this foreword, Si Kahn's tenure as executive director of Grassroots Leadership is about to come to an end. I am not sure whether he planned the publication of this book to coincide with his retirement, but what a wonderful way of transitioning toward and encouraging new leadership of the organization. Si has entitled his book "Creative Community Organizing," and his notion of leadership encourages experimentation and ingenuity rather than the hierarchical relations that we usually think about when "leadership" is at issue. He ends the chapter entitled "Don't Just Study History—Make It" with an imperative that captures the heart of creative leadership: "Whatever else, we must always be careful not to stand between the people we work with and their impossible dreams."

This is also, I think, the overarching theme of the book. A radically transformed social world—with affordable housing, health care for all, and free education, for example—might seem to be an unachievable aspiration. However, as Si points out, the abolition of slavery seemed, in its day, an unattainable ideal, but also there were activists who did not allow the weight of the present to prevent them from fighting for the release of black slaves from bondage. He makes the more general point with these powerful words:

> What I believe history does teach us is that in the broad struggle for justice you never really know what's possible and what's not. So, as creative community organizers, we need to be very careful not to limit the hopes and dreams of the people we work with. If we are not careful, our hardheaded "realism," historical "knowledge," and strategic "sensibility" may hold people back from taking on apparently unwinnable fights—that, if they are wise enough to ignore our advice, may instead turn out to be critical, deeply significant victories.

Within progressive circles, we have long wrestled with the meaning of cultural production and performance in relation to the mobilization of transformative mass movements and the development of radical political consciousness. Even though we frequently acknowledge that music, poetry, visual culture, and other modes of creative expression can play major roles in provoking new understandings of persisting social problems, we still tend to assume that it is through reasoned discourse—political analysis and speeches at rallies, for example—that the core issues related to social change are laid out. We assume that we fully learn, for example, through rational discourse, how to challenge homophobia and transphobia. It is also too frequently assumed that music, spoken word, guerrilla theater, film, etc. are simply important appendages to the ideas expressed in rational discourse, and can never be considered primary modes of political expression. These are the assumptions Si avidly disputes in *Creative Community Organizing*.

The key to understanding how Si Kahn envisions the role of culture in organizing for radical change resides in the significance of storytelling. He sees music, visual art, poetry, and theater as "the multiple methods human beings use to tell stories." Through these stories, we learn how to imagine ourselves as communities empowered to create change—to eradicate racism, anti-Semitism, sexism, and ableism, to overthrow homophobia, transphobia, and xenophobia. He argues that given the embeddedness of these ideologies and the material structures that anchor them, traditional political organizing cannot, by itself, succeed in forging genuine solidarity and community.

Thus Si Kahn relentlessly reminds us that building radical communities of struggle involves both the intellect and the emotions. The architecture of this book performs the very linkages of heart, mind, and spirit that he sees as the foundation of creative and effective organizing. The chapter entitled "Lift Every Voice," for example, tells the story of how he became an organizer and a songwriter and evokes the songwriters and singers he met, the places where he heard community singing, including black churches, where he listened to choirs singing the Negro National Anthem. We are moved by the stories he tells, we are transported by the lyrics he offers us, and we appreciate how a story about his own father's childhood in an Orthodox Jewish household can resonate far beyond that place and that moment. Having heard his father speak many times about being sent out by his mother every evening to forage for coal along the railroad tracks so that they would have a fire in the morning, Si assumed this was a story about poverty. But when he asked his father many years later about growing up poor, he was quickly corrected. Poor was not having enough to eat—and they had food on the table every day. This was a story about the triumph over poverty. This was a story about determination and dignity.

As an anti-prison activist for at least four decades, I deeply appreciate the care with which Si describes the campaigns Grassroots Leadership has undertaken against private, for-profit prisons, jails, and detention centers, and to end immigrant family detention, especially the incarceration of young children. Their challenges to private prisons have helped to generate new understandings of the extent to which high incarceration rates in the

United States—in fact the highest in the world, along with the largest numbers of imprisoned populations in the world—are a direct reflection of corporate stakes in an expanding prison system. Corrections Corporation of America—the company Grassroots Leadership has targeted on many occasions—is the global leader of private, for-profit prisons. Examining the history of CCA and its attempts to develop private prisons throughout the world for the sole purpose of generating more profit also helps us to understand the incursion of for-profit companies into virtually every aspect of the public prison process—including health care, food preparation, communications, and all the things 2.3 million human beings behind bars are allowed by their keepers to have. In struggling to end this privatization and corporatization of punishment, some of us dream of a social landscape that will no longer rely on the prison.

I have read this book with a particular interest in discovering modes of creative organizing that will assist us in building a broader campaign for prison abolition. Others will read it in search of approaches to other political issues, hoping to identify strategies for building the mass movements that can negotiate the contradictions of our times. I can guarantee you that everyone who reads this book will experience moments of enlightenment and will be deeply moved by Si Kahn's passion for justice and by his commitment never to stand between people and their impossible dreams.

Angela Davis
University of California, Santa Cruz

Introduction

I have been a radical for fifty years and more
Stood against the rich and greedy
For the workers and the poor
From Canada to Mexico I traveled everywhere
Wherever trouble called me, I was there
Like stitches in a crazy quilt that women piece and sew
Wherever there was suffering, I was bound to go
With angry words for cowardice, comfort for despair
Whenever help was needed, I was there

I was there in the depressions
When times were at their worst
But we had them where we wanted
Like a dam about to burst
With fire in our bellies, revolution in the air
For a moment we saw clearly—I was there
There were times I saw the issues
In quite a different light
And old friends turned against me
But I never left the fight
When stones were in my passway
And the road was far from clear
Whether I chose right or wrongly, I was there

On a day when hope goes hungry
And your dreams seem bound to fall
You may see me at the mill
Or just outside the union hall
When the clouds are empty promises
The sky a dark despair
Like an eagle from the mountain, I'll be there
And you, my brave young comrades,
When the future sounds the call
Will you be there for the battle,
Will you answer, one and all
When the roll is called up yonder
When the roll's called anywhere
Will you stand and answer proudly, "We're still here"
Will you stand and answer proudly, "I was there"

I wrote this song some years ago as a tribute to Mother Jones, the great labor radical, famously called "the most dangerous woman in America." But, aside from the hyperbole (Mother Jones was not exactly renowned for her modesty, and I would never describe myself, as I believe she might easily have done, as "an eagle from the mountains"—totem animal-wise, I'm more of a stubborn dog that won't let go of a bone), it could easily be about me.

I have indeed been a radical "for fifty years and more," and proudly so. For forty-five of my almost sixty-six years, I've made my living as a professional civil rights, labor, and community organizer.

It was my great good fortune to begin my organizing career as a volunteer with the Student Nonviolent Coordinating Committee (SNCC), the militant student wing of the Southern Civil Rights Movement. SNCC (pronounced "SNICK") was nothing if not creative. Drawing on old traditions of African American resistance, shaped by veterans of the civil rights, labor, and peace movements, it developed not only ways of thinking about how community organizing can change the world for the better, but also strategies to make that real in the world. The great movements of the last forty-five years—among them those of women, workers, welfare recipients, peace lovers, students, lesbian, bisexual, gay, transgender and queer/questioning activists, union members, and environmentalists—would not have been what they were without the influence and lessons of the Southern Civil Rights Movement.

Most organizers spend their entire hard-working lives without ever being lucky enough to take part in a campaign or movement that gets noted by history. I have had the great good fortune to have been involved with five of them: In the 1960s, I joined the Southern Civil Rights Movement. In the 1970s and early 1980s, I was involved in the Brookside Strike, led by the United Mine Workers of America (UMWA) in Harlan County, Kentucky; the J. P. Stevens Campaign for unionization in the southern textile mills, led by the Amalgamated Clothing and Textile Workers Union (ACTWU); and the Brown Lung Movement, in which cotton mill workers disabled by the deadly disease known medically as byssinosis fought for compensation and to clean up the mills. Since the mid-1990s, Grassroots Leadership, the organization I've worked for over the last thirty years, has led the national campaign to abolish all for-profit private prisons, jails, and detention centers, and to put an end to immigrant family detention, the appalling recent practice in which children as young as infants are imprisoned together with their parents.

I don't deal with all these campaigns and movements in this book. Rather, I've chosen to write the way my grandmothers cooked, "a little of this, a little of that," to create a smorgasbord rather than a history, either of organizing or of my own life and work.

As with any trade, there is an established way to do community organizing, basic principles and skills that you'll find in any organizer's toolbox. A number of handbooks and strategy manuals lay all of this out, including my own earlier books *How People Get Power* and *Organizing: A Guide for Grassroots Leaders*. Pick up any of them, and you'll learn the common wisdom of generations of organizers, along with the shoptalk of the trade: one-on-ones, door knocking, strategy sessions, shift meetings, tactics, actions, accountability sessions, free media, negotiations.

That's not what this book is about. Rather, it deals with creative variations on the general theme of organizing. What distinguished the campaigns and movements in which I was involved was their creativity. I've spent my working life learning from the best—literally hundreds of civil rights, labor, and community organizers who brought not just passion and courage but great freshness and innovation to everything they did.

That's why this book is titled *Creative Community Organizing*. It's a tribute to all of the wonderful organizers with whom I've worked and shared stories over these forty-five years, a praise song to the traditions of activism and resistance we share, and that we work to pass on to the next generations of "rabble-rousers, activists, and quiet lovers of justice."

Because I'm not just an organizer, but also a historian, songwriter, and storyteller, I believe that a straight line is often the longest distance between two points. It's true that, as the saying goes, "If you don't know where you're going, any road will get you there."

But even if you have a clear destination in mind, it doesn't necessarily follow that the best way to get there is the shortest. You'll find that attitude reflected in the winding road that is this book, with lots of detours and side trips along the way. But, as creative community organizers, we do know where we're going—and we will get there.

In my own work as an organizer, I've tried to "keep my eyes on the prize," to stay focused on the goal, the victory that will give the people I'm working with changes for the better that they can see and feel. But I'm also concerned with what people learn on the way to that victory: about themselves, each other, history, justice, community, friendship. I want them to love the struggle for justice, not endure it.

So I've written this book the way I organize. Think of creative community organizing as a highway leading to somewhere you passionately want to go, but with lots of interesting side roads and paths to explore along the way. When in the course of this book you hit a song, a story, a poem, a bit of oral history, think of it as a chance to turn off the main drag for a little while, to rest yourself from the journey, to feel as well as to think.

As a historian, I tend to pay attention to the path behind as well as the road ahead. Because I want history to be accessible to a wide range of people who have different relationships to reading, I've used songs in my organizing as a way to tell stories. I am always moved and inspired when everyday people decide not just to read history but to make it, so it's their stories that so many of my songs are about.

The lyrics you'll encounter are taken from songs I wrote. If someone else wrote one of the poems or songs that salt the book, I'll tell you in the text who they are.

Why did I write this book? Almost every day, I encounter people who have a passionate desire to make a difference in the world, to do whatever it takes to change it for the better. Like the phototropic plants that grow towards the light, they lean towards doing what is right, often at considerable risk and cost. Dr. Martin Luther King Jr. said that "the arc of the moral universe . . . bends towards justice." So do individual people—and they are the salt of the earth.

My greatest hope is that when one of these natural-born activists says to someone who's been organizing for years, "So do you think I should become an organizer?" they'll tell them about this book and say, "Read it, then come back and talk with me."

I can't tell you whether you should become an organizer, full time or volunteer, although I hope many of you who read *Creative*

Community Organizing will decide it's something that makes sense for you. I will just say that I cannot imagine any work that would have given me a better life and a stronger sense of having done my best to make a difference, not just for those with whom I've worked, but for myself.

As Mother Jones says in the song, "Whether I chose right or wrongly, I was there."

Unite the Divided, Divide the United

Have you heard of General Nathan Bedford Forrest
For five years he fought the Yankees hand to hand
But after Appomattox he got lonesome
So he went and organized the Ku Klux Klan
His ex-soldiers crossed the Mississippi River
And founded Forrest City, Arkansas
I never got to meet old General Forrest
But then he never met my old friend, Mervin Barr

All along the bars and grills of Forrest City
Talking to the people where they are
"I think it's time for us to get together
There's no need to be afraid," says Mervin Barr
Shooting pool to supplement the pension
From injuries he got in the Marines
When he talked, you couldn't help but listen
He was the gentlest man I've ever seen

Some days he was too sick to leave the Southside
Where he lived with his Momma
In a little old shotgun shack
So they'd take him to the VA home in Memphis
Where the sheets were white,
But Mervin's face was black

But he knew that he was needed by his people
And he marched them up and down that Delta town
The doctors tried to send him back to Memphis
But he wouldn't leave until the fight was won

They say that on the day that he was buried
Five hundred people stood beside his grave
I don't like funerals, but I kind of wish I'd been there
Though I couldn't say just why I feel that way
The nightriders' shotguns didn't kill him
Nor the people who had sworn they'd do him in
He died because he wouldn't go to Memphis
And I don't expect to see his like again

I learned a lot the summer I turned twenty-one.

I learned to eat catfish, grits, collard greens, country ham with red eye gravy, and streak o'lean sandwiches.

I learned there's such a thing as community organizing, and that, with good teachers, just about anyone can learn to do it creatively.

I learned that everyday people have a great capacity for building unity across the lines that so often divide them, especially when they have an organizer helping them learn how.

I learned that the institutions and people that hold power over others are rarely as united as they first appear.

I learned that, with a little creativity, an experienced organizer can help people work to widen the cracks that separate powerful people and institutions from each other, and win victories that change their own lives for the better.

I learned the meaning of courage.

I had missed the famous Mississippi Summer of 1964, when thousands of volunteers went to that state to help its African American residents become citizens in the full sense of the word: people who could register to vote, go to the polls on election day, and mark a paper ballot for the candidates of their choice. I wanted to go South for what everyone knew would be an important moment in history, but my parents quite literally feared for my life and refused to let me go.

At the time, I thought my folks were paranoid, arbitrary, and unreasonable. Today, almost fifty years later—now that Elizabeth Minnich and I have raised three children—I'm willing to admit they had a point.

Here's what led to Mississippi Summer. During the Reconstruction years that followed the end of the Civil War, with male former slaves now having the right to vote, more than fifteen hundred African Americans were elected to public office in the states of the former Confederacy. Under their leadership, most states in the South for the first time established public schools and passed some of the most progressive legislation in the country at that time. Black and white teachers traveled from the North to help the ex-slaves learn to read and write. Mississippi and South Carolina elected the first Black members of Congress in this country's history.

For most white southerners, this only added insult to injury. When in 1877, President Rutherford B. Hayes withdrew the federal troops that had occupied the South since the end of the Civil War, these white southerners struck back with full force. The states that had been part of the Confederacy began systematically, violently, to deny Black people the right to vote and, along with that, virtually anything else that might be considered a right. African Americans who even attempted to register to vote were harassed, intimidated, beaten, run out of town, shot, lynched.

"White supremacy," as that system proudly called itself, meant exactly that. Within a few years, throughout the South, virtually every elected and appointed official was again white: sheriffs, police chiefs, county commissioners, mayors, city council members, judges, district attorneys, jailers, school superintendents, principals, county agricultural agents, welfare department heads. So were almost all the people who held economic power: plantation owners, factory operators, landlords, large farmers, bankers, to name just a few.

The white South, as it turned out, hadn't really lost the Civil War (which in many parts of the South is still called the War Between the States and, in Charleston, South Carolina, so help me, "The War of Northern Aggression"). It had simply been defeated in some battles between 1861 and 1865, suffered through a relatively brief period of federal military occupation and Black political power, and then, as its leaders had always promised, had risen again.

For white people to stay on top required keeping Black people on the bottom. Here the vote was key. The Reconstruction experience had shown the potential for Black political mobilization, especially in South Carolina and Mississippi, the two states with African American majorities. Elections in which Blacks participated freely could, at least in those areas, do severe damage to white supremacy as a political if not an economic system. No fools, the South's white leaders did their level best to make sure that would never happen.

Then, after more than a century of organizing by African Americans all over the United States, supported by allies of other races and ethnicities, Congress passed the Voting Rights Act of 1965. It was a promise to Black people in the South that they could finally register and vote without fear of intimidation, retaliation, violence, death.

The summer volunteers went to Mississippi in 1964, even before the Voting Rights Act was passed, to work to make that promise real. I followed them in the newspapers and on our black-and-white TV, wishing I were there. I swore as soon as I turned twenty-one, I would follow in their footsteps.

To my amazement then and now, I actually did. I was lucky enough to have a car that was only twelve years old—a 1953 Chevy my Uncle Charlie had given me after its owner, my Aunt Reba, died too young of cancer. In early May 1965, less than two weeks after my twenty-first birthday, I loaded up a few belongings, the thirteen-dollar Kamico guitar I had been given for my Bar Mitzvah, my fishing gear and my tools, and headed south. Because I had skills as a carpenter and auto mechanic, I had been accepted as a volunteer by the Student Nonviolent Coordinating Committee, known popularly—or, by most southern whites, unpopularly—as SNCC.

I view my arrival in Arkansas in the early summer of 1965 as the moment when I discovered what I was meant to do in this world: to help people learn how to work together to help change it for the better.

During my first fifteen years, as a kid growing up in a small college town in central Pennsylvania, just beyond the edge of the anthracite coal fields, I never thought very much about the ways the world worked. Like so many people who haven't been politicized, I thought things were the way they were. Things happened—they weren't made to happen. If something changed, for the better or for the worse, it was just because it had changed. I don't think I had any real sense of cause and effect—or knew that, all over the world, organizers were working strategically to help people challenge and change injustice.

I found out soon enough about the world of creative community organizing. After a week's training in Little Rock, I was sent to Forrest City, on the Arkansas side of the Mississippi River Delta, about forty miles west of Memphis. As anyone in Forrest City, Black or white, would tell you, the town was founded by former Confederate cavalry leader General Nathan Bedford Forrest. Bitter in defeat, he vowed revenge and became an early leader of the Ku Klux Klan as a means to that end. From everything I could see and hear in Forrest City, the white leadership of the town was doing their best to live up to its namesake's legacy.

I got my first lesson in creative community organizing early. The department stores in Forrest City made most of their money from Black customers, but every employee on the floor was white. There were some Black employees working where you couldn't see them, in the stock rooms and on the loading docks. But no African American had ever in the history of Forrest City run a cash register in a white-owned store. As far as the good white leaders of the town were concerned, no Black person ever would.

When I arrived, the local SNCC project leaders had just decided to take on this issue. Knowing that the department stores would say they couldn't find any African Americans who were qualified to operate a cash register, the organizers had started a training program. To help persuade the store owners to hire some of the trainees once they graduated from the program, they also decided to start a boycott.

I knew just enough about boycotts to ask, "So you're going to boycott all the white merchants in town?"

No, one of the SNCC veterans explained. Since virtually all the merchants were white, that would leave the African American community with no place to get the basics they needed to survive. The nearest towns were at least thirty miles away and, being smaller than Forrest City, charged higher prices. Though the local merchants were willing to extend some credit to their Black customers (at outrageous interest rates, to be sure), stores in other towns would want customers from outside their county—especially Black ones—to pay cash.

Why not go to Memphis, I asked, where there were lots of Black-owned businesses and prices were lower than in the small towns of the Delta?

The SNCC regulars had an answer for everything. Not enough Black residents of Forrest City and surrounding St. Francis County owned vehicles. If they did have a car or truck, it was likely to be even older and in worse shape than my '53 Chevy. Plus gas was high—whatever they saved in Memphis would be lost filling up the tank.

"All right," I said. "How about organizing a carpool, or using one of the church buses to take folks to Memphis to shop?"

The SNCC leaders were remarkably patient in the face of my persistent questions and suggestions. I didn't realize it at the time, but they were being both kind and strategic. Part of their job was to take the raw recruits like me who had come to volunteer and turn us into organizers.

I must have been quite a challenge. One of the keys to successful organizing, they explained, is simplicity. The more complicated a strategy or tactic, the harder it is to carry out and the less likely it will be successful. You can ask one person to do a lot of things, particularly if they're a seasoned, committed activist. But if you want hundreds or thousands of people to participate in a campaign, you need to ask the great majority of them to do one thing, and only one.

I wasn't used to thinking like this, but I was learning fast. "So, basically," I said, "we should only boycott the four department stores." I was pleased with myself for figuring this out.

No, wrong again. If we boycotted all four stores, we'd force them into a position of solidarity with each other. They'd each be losing comparable amounts of business, so they'd oppose the boycott with equal force. They'd sit down and strategize together, create a united front, get support from other merchants and the local power structure—and use that base to retaliate against the Black community.

In other words, by boycotting all the stores at once, we'd be helping unite them, when our goal should be to divide them.

The best way to do that was to boycott only one of the four stores, doing our best to shut it down, until and unless the owners agreed to hire their first Black cashier. That way, no one in the African American community really had to give up anything in order to support the boycott. They could shop at any of the other three department stores. They just couldn't shop at the one being boycotted. The store owners would be divided, while the Black community was united in their shared effort to win jobs and justice.

Doing it this way, the SNCC veterans continued, would split the power structure. The three department store owners who weren't being boycotted would be getting business from the regular customers of the boycotted store—the organizers and Black community leaders would see to that. The longer the boycott went on, the greater the chance that these customers would switch their loyalty to another store permanently.

In this situation, the owners of the three stores not being boycotted would have little incentive to fight back, or to encourage other white business owners and community leaders to do so. By isolating one store, instead of taking on the whole town at once, we would increase our chance of victory.

Meanwhile, the owner of the store being boycotted, the "target" (I was also learning organizing shoptalk), would have to stare out the window all day, watching his customers go over to his competitors while his own sales sank lower and lower.

Brilliant! I was starting to understand how all this worked, just how thoughtful and skillful my organizing teachers were.

So which of the department stores were we going to boycott?

The "Jew store."

I froze.

Let it be said that I was the only Jew on the Forrest City SNCC staff. For all I knew, I was the only Jew in St. Francis County, maybe even in the entire Delta. Hell, I could have been the only Jew in Arkansas—with the exception of the solitary department store owner.

I understood that the other department store owners might not feel the same sense of kinship with a Jewish businessperson that they would with a Christian one, less likely to stretch out a hand in hard times—and vice versa, if the situation had been reversed. But to pick on the one Jewish store in town didn't seem quite fair. SNCC was fighting for the ultimate underdog, African Americans.

To target another historic underdog, even if one more privileged than his Black customers—didn't that just reinforce the injustice?

I was not just learning how to do creative community organizing. I was being introduced to its ethical complications.

~~~

It does have to be said that, almost certainly out of my discomfort with the decision to boycott the one Jewish store in Forrest City, I walked that particular picket line less often than I should have. Mr. White, on the other hand, never missed a day.

Every one of the Forrest City SNCC workers was in awe of Mr. White's courage. Not only was he in his late eighties or early nineties, he was blind.

The picket line wasn't an easy place to be. Carloads and truckloads of rough-looking young and not-so-young whites drove by at high speeds, screaming obscenities, swerving suddenly as if they were going to drive straight into the line.

Mr. White kept walking.

White police officers stood spread-legged across the street, staring, one hand on the butts of their automatic pistols, the other on their billy clubs, eyes hidden behind their cop-size silver shades, faces frozen with anger and hate, just waiting for an excuse to do what they couldn't stand not doing.

Mr. White kept walking.

The mid-day Delta sun felt like it was about to burn a hole clear through the concrete. Sweat ran down the faces and arms of the picketers like small streams, hit the sidewalk with a hiss, turned into steam, and disappeared.

Mr. White kept walking.

I wasn't at the picket line the day it happened, but I sure heard about it. Everybody in Forrest City and surrounding St. Francis County heard about it. By nightfall, the story had probably traveled halfway to Little Rock and back.

What happened was that one of the other picketers went up to Mr. White and said, "Mr. White, I just want to thank you for inspiring us all with your courage. Here you are, old and blind. Yet you just keep going, hour after hour, day after day, walking for freedom. Why aren't you afraid?"

Mr. White stopped for a moment. He leaned hard on his white cane with one hand to steady himself, put the other hand in his pocket, and said, "I'm not afraid, because I've got . . . ""

I need to pause briefly here. Ninety-nine times out of a hundred, when southerners, Black or white, start a sentence with, "I'm not afraid, because I've got . . . ," they end that same sentence with "Jesus," "God," "My Jesus," "My God," or some combination or slight variation thereof, followed by "with me," "walking with me," "watching over me," "by my side," or—you get the idea.

"I'm not afraid, because I've got . . . this," Mr. White concluded, pulling an ancient owl-head revolver out of his pocket, leveling it, and swinging it around in every direction.

I have never before or after heard of a picket line scattering so fast.

~~~

I also wasn't at the picket line the day Vincent O'Connor came over from one of the other local SNCC projects to help out. Vince was a Catholic Worker, something else I was learning about for the first time. The Catholic Worker Movement was started in 1932 by Dorothy Day, a radical pacifist who believed in serving the poor by living and working among them. Today, there are 185 Catholic Worker houses all over the world, where people of conscience live out the values of their faith.

On the day that Vince O'Connor joined the picket line, one of the screeching trucks didn't just swerve. It screamed to a stop next to the line. A man stormed out, his white face red with rage, a .45 automatic in his hand. He walked up to Vince and stuck the pistol in his stomach.

I don't know what the man said to Vince, but you can imagine. The local whites were angry enough at their longtime African American neighbors, who after generations of forced subservience were finally standing up to them. But they reserved their most livid, uncontrollable rage for the white civil rights workers—the southerners in particular (they, of all people, should know better), with those from anywhere else not far behind.

To these angry women and men of Forrest City, the white SNCC workers were "race traitors," "race mixers," "Negro lovers" (although that wasn't exactly the phrase they used). By breaking ranks with the other white people who were shouting, "Segregation now, segregation tomorrow, segregation forever," and by insisting on the rights and common humanity of our Black sisters and brothers, we were tearing a hole in the myth of white supremacy, challenging what southern whites saw as "our sacred way of life." Not surprisingly, they hated us.

All the time the man was screaming at Vince O'Connor, his pistol pushed hard against Vince's stomach, Vince stood quietly. When the man finally stopped, Vince looked at him sadly, shook his head, and said simply, "I'm sorry you feel that way."

Then he just stood there, waiting. The other SNCC workers who saw it said it seemed like time stopped.

Finally, the man cursed, spun around, stomped back to his truck, and drove off.

I had no experience with the kind of courage that Mr. White and Vincent O'Connor had shown on that department store picket line. I'm still amazed that anyone could do what they did. I don't think I have that kind of courage in me.

Vincent O'Connor and Mr. White weren't the only ones who taught me about courage that summer. Mervin Barr was a young ex-Marine, twenty-seven years old, who left the service on disability after being beaten so badly by white Marines that his kidneys had been permanently damaged. He shuttled back and forth between his mother's house in Forrest City and the Veterans Administration hospital in Memphis, some forty-five miles to the east.

He knew he was living on borrowed time and decided to make the most of it. He spent much of every day walking all over Forrest City, encouraging every Black person he met to come by the Freedom Center, to register to vote, to show up at the mass meeting that night at Clay's Funeral Home.

To the young people in Forrest City, Mervin Barr was a hero. To the older people, he was something of a problem. An excellent pool player, he spent a lot of time working the tables, picking up a little extra cash to supplement his meager Marine Corps disability payment.

The tables, needless to say, were located in pool halls and bars. To those who constituted Forrest City's Black middle class—teachers, preachers, small-business owners, independent farmers—that wasn't the image of African American leadership they wanted to project. For years they had performed a delicate and often courageous balancing act, working to meet the needs of and provide leadership to the Black community while trying not to alienate powerful white community leaders whose relative goodwill in large part determined how much progress was possible for Blacks.

But these established leaders also wanted to protect their own power, access, and privilege, limited though it may have been. For years, when the white leaders of Forrest City had a message they wanted to communicate to the African American community, or something they needed from it, these leaders had been called on to play that role. Some of them were even now, almost certainly at the demand of the white leadership, communicating a go-slow message to the rest of the Black community.

Go slow was hardly what the Black high school students and dropouts who hung around the Freedom Center wanted to hear. As far as they were concerned, African Americans had waited far too long already, almost three hundred and fifty years. Freedom some day in the far future was no longer good enough. They resonated to the message they heard from Mervin Barr: "Freedom now!"

I was discovering another important organizing principle: No matter how much any group, any constituency, is confronted with a common problem that unites its members in some ways, they will be divided in others. If they are of the same race, they may still be split by class, gender, religion, sexual orientation—any of the many different ways in which people can divide themselves into artificial "kinds" and away from each other.

It's all well and good to chant, "The people united/Will never be defeated/El pueblo unido/jamás será vencido." But, in real life and campaigns for justice, the people are always partly united, partly divided. It's up to the organizers working with them to understand that this will always be the case and to do whatever we can to reinforce the unity and compensate for the divisions among the people with whom we work. Our job as organizers is to divide the united—the people and institutions who hold power over others—and to unite the divided—the dispossessed, disempowered people with whom we work, who should command our deepest loyalty and fiercest commitment.

~~~

I was back North when I got the news. I don't remember who called me, but it was a simple message.

"Mervin Barr is dead," the voice said.

"Who got him?" I asked. I was sure it was the Klan, or someone from the Forrest City police or the St. Francis County sheriff's office—the same thing as the Klan, in many cases.

"It was his kidneys. By the time they got him back to the hospital, it was too late."

I didn't understand. "I thought he had that under control."

The voice was low and sad. "He did, as long as he went to the VA hospital twice a week. But he stopped going."

"Why?" I couldn't believe he was so suddenly gone.

"He knew we needed him. He didn't want to leave us."

There is the courage to walk a picket line day after day, listening to the shouts, the taunts, the scream of the engine, the screech of the tires, not knowing if and when a careening truck will deliberately jump the curb and plow into the line of march, carrying you with it.

There is the courage of standing absolutely still while someone pushes an automatic pistol into your stomach, and waiting silently while they decide whether to pull the trigger.

There is the quiet heroism of doing your work day after day, of taking care of others before you take care of yourself—the courage of deciding that sometimes there are things more important than life itself, and that Freedom is one of them.

If You Don't fight, You Lose Every Time

Stones in the furrow, rocks in the field
Can't hardly keep the plow from breaking
I could be there riding all around these fields
Boss of any thing worth taking
Shotgun on my shoulder, whip in my hand
Keep the mule in the furrow
And the cropper on the land

Stones in the graveyard, rocks in the fence
Surround the bones of those who bore me
I can see their faces rising up like questions
All along the road before me
With nothing to count on
But their hard-working hands
They were trampled like the cotton
And broken like the land

Stones in the pathway, rocks in the road
My friends and family have to travel
If I go with them, if I go against them
How will they speak my name tomorrow
All you can count on when your final crop comes in
Is the harvest that gets gathered
By your neighbors and your kin

Even if you're broken, at least you won't be shamed
You know some day your children
Will be proud to say your name
On this old river, on this plantation
In this dark season, on this long night

*P*resident Lyndon Baines John-
son signed the Voting Rights Act of 1965 into law on August 6.
It was designed to make real the Fifteenth Amendment to the
Constitution, passed in 1870. "The right of citizens of the United
States to vote," that law says, "shall not be denied or abridged by
the United States or by any State on account of race, color, or
previous condition of servitude."

That sentence inspired hope in millions of African Americans
who had only recently been slaves. But they were fighting words
to most southern whites, who fully understood what that change
would mean for them.

So, having been defeated in war, the white South did its best
to achieve victory during peacetime, using threats, intimidation,
and violence, up to and including thousands of lynchings, to stop
attempts by Blacks to register and vote.

It isn't enough for a law to be on the books. It has to be real on
the streets. The Fifteenth Amendment, for most southern African
Americans, might as well have been written on the wind.

So the leaders of SNCC decided to test whether the Voting
Rights Act of 1965 meant what it said, by going up and down the
streets in Forrest City's African American neighborhoods, trying
to get as many people as we could to register to vote.

One desperately hot afternoon in late August, working my
way down one of the dusty back streets on the Black side of town,
I stopped by a small house. An ancient-looking woman was rocking on the porch.

"Good afternoon, Ma'am," I said.

She nodded and kept rocking.

"I'm from the Freedom Center," I went on. "I wonder if I could talk with you for a minute or two?"

She nodded again and gestured towards a straight-backed chair opposite her. I sat down. I really wanted to ask how old she was, but it didn't seem the polite thing to do.

She must have guessed my question. "You know," she said, "I was born a slave."

In my forty-five years as an organizer, there are a very few moments when I felt I was in the presence of some kind of special grace.

"I was four years old when we got freed."

I didn't know what to say. I just sat there, in wonder, speechless.

The woman who had been born a slave reached out to me. "How can I help you?"

She had rescued me. "Ma'am, the president of the United States has signed a law saying that everyone has the right to vote."

She cut me off, gently. "I read the papers. Every day. I know."

"I was hoping you'd go with me to the courthouse to register to vote."

She stopped rocking and leaned forward.

"Son," she said, "I'm 106 years old. I don't leave my rocking chair."

I was caught between figuring out what year that meant she'd been born and trying to frame a response. All I could come up with was, "If you didn't have to leave your rocking chair, would you register to vote?" It was half a nervous joke. I didn't know what else to say.

"I would," she said. "But I don't ever leave my rocking chair."

I went back to the Freedom Center. As usual, there were a number of young Black men there, some doing different kinds of volunteer work, others just enjoying this one piece of liberated territory in the midst of Forrest City. Still in awe at having sat and talked with someone who had been born a slave, I told them what I'd just seen and heard.

One of the Michigan locals of the United Auto Workers union had sent the Forrest City SNCC project a brand-new bright yellow four-on-the-floor three-quarter-ton Dodge pickup. One of the young men took the keys from where they hung on a nail by the front door and slid into the driver's seat. The others climbed into the cab or the back of the truck.

They drove to where her house was located and stepped together onto the porch.

They lifted her, still in her rocking chair, carried her outside, and placed her, chair and all, in the back of the truck.

With the young men in the back kneeling next to her, each with a hand on the chair to steady it, they drove as slowly as they could, weaving their way through the Black community, up one street and down another: past the churches and the adjacent graveyards, the segregated elementary school and high school, the little grocery stores, Clay's Funeral Home, and the Freedom Center.

As word spread, people poured out onto their porches, into their yards, to watch as she passed, sitting straight and proud in her chair, in the back of the bright yellow pickup they all recognized on sight. Everyone knew who she was, the eldest member of their community, the woman who had been born a slave—and they knew where she was going.

When there was no street untraveled, no place in the Black community left to trumpet the news, the young men turned towards the courthouse, parking directly in front of the entrance, where everyone passing by could see them.

Then they carried her in that throne up the courthouse steps and into the registrar's office, so she could register to vote.

If that isn't Freedom, what is?

$\sim\!\sim$

Where had this wonderful spirit of resistance come from? Forrest City, Arkansas, lies in the center of St. Francis County, named for the river that runs through it. Like that other great river into which it flows, the Mississippi, the St. Francis River flooded regularly. Over centuries, the earth surrounding it grew deep and dark for miles in every direction.

In 1965 and for hundreds of years before that, in spring along the St. Francis River, you could see thousands of sharecroppers and tenant farmers, Black and white, their hoes rising and falling in a long cadence as they chopped the cotton, cutting down the weeds that would otherwise choke the young plants. In fall, those same hands were back in the fields, pulling the now mature bolls away from the bract, the hard shell that lies underneath each white puff, stuffing the cotton into the sacks they dragged behind them down the long rows.

It was back-breaking, badly paying, poor people's work. From time to time, the poor people stood up and fought back. In 1919, African American tenant farmers and sharecroppers in Phillips County, just to the southeast, organized a union, inspired partly by new attitudes and perceptions that Black veterans brought back from the battlefields of World War I. The response by whites was the Elaine Massacre, a violent armed attack on the Black community, in which hundreds of African Americans were murdered.

White sharecroppers and tenant farmers had also tried to organize. They had even gotten as far as a strike, broken when the plantation owners brought in African Americans to pick the cotton.

Over time, Blacks and whites came to the same conclusion. Whatever hatreds and resentments they bore, when it came to organizing to change their wages and working conditions, they needed each other.

The tiny village of Tyronza is just about forty miles north and a little west of Forrest City. One night in July of 1934, seven African American and eleven white men met secretly, under cover of darkness, in the Sunnyside School. The school was on the boundary of land belonging to Hiram Norcross, who had kicked twenty-three tenant farmers and their families off his land that spring. They pledged that they would no longer accept twenty cents for their labor, but would organize a Southern Tenant Farmers' Union and demand a dollar for every hundred pounds of cotton they picked.

When the plantation owners laughed, the union called a strike, Black and white together. The planters hit back with evictions and violence, much of it instigated by the Knights of the White Camellia, the local variety of the Ku Klux Klan.

By the time the planters gave in and agreed to pay what the strikers demanded, an estimated thirty thousand sharecroppers and tenant farmers up and down the east side of Arkansas had folded their arms, laid down their tools, and refused to pick cotton. The strike and the Southern Tenant Farmers' Union had become an international cause. The Socialist Party sent its president Norman Thomas to Arkansas and took on the responsibility of fundraising to help the evicted workers, now living in tent cities along the highways. The British Labor Party sent two of its senior women activists as official observers.

I learned this history long after I left Forrest City and St. Francis County from H. L. Mitchell, the white former tenant farmer who had been the union's president. Only twenty-six years had passed between the great strike and when I arrived. Some of the Black farmers with whom I spent time must have been part of it. Given how often in community organizing past experience leads to future action, some of them must have been among the leaders of the Black farmers' cooperative SNCC was now helping to organize.

But no one ever said a word to me. Perhaps the memories of the long years that followed that sweet moment of victory, in which the union was effectively broken, and so many of its members and leaders driven from the Delta, were just too bitter. Maybe this just wasn't the kind of information you volunteered to a white stranger, even a SNCC worker. Maybe it was just that I didn't know enough to ask the right questions.

Whatever the explanation, by the time I arrived in East Arkansas in 1965, memories of that brief moment of racial solidarity had been repressed and, at least publicly, forgotten. Once again, the line that divided Black and white ran as straight and true as a long row of cotton.

~~~

If it was hard getting the authorities to enforce local laws, when it came to federal statutes, it was as if the South had never rejoined the Union.

I got to Forrest City a year after the passage of the federal Public Accommodations Act of 1964, one of the historic pieces of legislation forced through Congress by the Civil Rights Movement. Beyond all the legalese, what it said was that if any enterprise served the public, it had to *serve the public.* It couldn't serve only the white public and not the Black public. It had to serve everybody.

Today we would say, "What part of 'serve the public' don't you understand?"

This apparently simple message was having a hard time getting a hearing among white Arkansans. So, being creative community organizers, the SNCC project leaders decided to speed things up a little.

"We've got you down for the Wagon Wheel," one of them told me. This was not good news. The parking lot of the edge-of-town barbecue joint regularly sported more rebel flags than a Confederate re-enactors' reunion.

"Fred will be parked across the street in case there's trouble." Fred was a white volunteer from one of the other projects, come to Forrest City for the day to bolster our meager forces.

"What's he going to do if there's trouble?"

"He'll drive back to the Freedom Center and let us know."

Okay, at least there was a plan.

Half a dozen African American teenagers piled into my Chevy. Young as they were, they were all seasoned veterans, trained and tested in nonviolence.

We walked in and crowded together at one table. Half a dozen sullen young whites sat at a table just across the aisle from us. I recognized one of them as Pat, who occasionally waited on me at the lumber yard.

I nodded at him. He didn't nod back.

The waitress came over, pad in hand. "What do you want?" she asked.

We'd agreed in advance that we'd all have ice cream. The goal was to test the Public Accommodations Act, to see if we'd be served—not to linger over a full meal while a crowd of angry whites gathered outside, as was so often the case. One by one, the teenagers ordered.

"I'd like a hot fudge sundae," I said.

The waitress dropped her pad to her side and shook her head. "The law says we've got to serve *them*," she said. "We don't have to serve *you*."

They ate. I paid up. We started to the door. Outside, one of Forrest City's largest was waiting.

"You!" he screamed, pointing at me. He'd picked up a log from the hickory pile that fed the barbecue fire and was holding it in one massive hand. "What kind of ice cream do you like?"

It seemed, under the circumstances, a strange question. I couldn't figure out how to respond.

"You like *chocolate*, don't you? You like *chocolate*." He spat the word out of his mouth like it was a piece of gristle he'd bitten down on in his barbecue sandwich.

I was still trying to figure out what he meant—okay, I'm slow sometimes—when he hit me. I think it was his fist rather than the hickory stick, but I'll never know for sure.

Regardless, I woke up in the back seat of Fred's car, my broken nose bleeding like the proverbial stuck pig. There were just the two of us in the car. "Where are the kids?" I was near panic.

"Don't worry. We got them out," Fred said. "They're okay."

"That's good." I relaxed a little bit. "Are we going to the Freedom Center? We need to tell them there's trouble."

Fred turned and looked at me strangely. "Don't worry," he finally said. "They know. Believe me, they know."

Check Your Stereotypes at the Door

I read in the paper, I watched on the show
They said that it happened a long time ago
The years had gone by, I just didn't know
　　　　Working for freedom now
The songs that we sang still ring in my ears
The hope and the glory, the pain and the fears
I just can't believe it's been forty-five years
　　　　Working for freedom now

Those who have fallen and given their last
Have passed on to us what remains of their task
To fight for the future and pray for the past
　　　　Working for freedom now
The song of their laughter, the sound of their feet
The voice of their pain that cries out in our sleep
Will be judged in the end by the faith that we keep
　　　　Working for freedom now

The wind in the winter is bitter and chill
The cries of the hunted are heard on the hill
I just can't believe there's such suffering still
　　　　Working for freedom now

The wind blows the summer from fields far away
We stand in the dust in the heat of the day
Our hearts stopped so still that there's nothing to say
Working for freedom now

Been a long time, but I keep on trying
For I know where I am bound
Been a hard road, but I don't mind dying
I have seen freedom

*I*n SNCC, we never called the great uprising of which we were a part the "Civil Rights Movement." What African Americans in the South and their allies called it was "The Freedom Movement," usually abbreviated to simply "the Movement."

A lot of songs from that period talk about "freedom." But, as far as I know, there aren't any that include the phrase "civil rights." When Black people talked about the Movement, they meant not just rights, but liberation.

The decision to use the term "civil rights" on the national scene was deliberate and strategic. It was hard for anyone to argue against the proposition that every person living in the United States should be able to enjoy the rights promised them by the Constitution. The phrase itself was dry, abstract, legalistic—not the sort of thing to keep white middle Americans awake at night.

Make no mistake: Rights, civil rights, public rights are critically important, particularly in a constitutional democracy, a society at least theoretically based on the rule of law. As public/feminist philosopher Elizabeth Minnich writes in our coauthored book, *The Fox in the Henhouse: How Privatization Threatens Democracy*:

People who are enslaved have no public life, no rights. They cannot go where they will, do what they will, say what they will. Because as slaves they have no public standing, they also have no private life. They have no place of their own, no doors they have a right to shut to protect their privacy. Slaves were raped and "bred" and their children taken from them. Not being public "persons," they also could not legally marry. They were vulnerable to intrusion at all times: no public life, no private life. . . . Some slave owners treated their slaves, their private property, better than others. But they did not have to. Those who have no public rights can only hope for mercy. They cannot demand justice.

The Civil Rights Movement was in part about making sure that southern African Americans could demand justice out loud, in public. It did this, though, not by creating special rights for them, but by dismantling the barriers of legal segregation, of American apartheid, that prevented Black people in the South from exercising the rights that others in this country had held for years.

But access to rights does not in and of itself create opportunity. Rather, it creates the opportunity for opportunity—for organizing that turns possibility into reality. The fact that there are today, in the South and throughout the United States, Black mayors, Black state legislators, Black members of Congress, a Black president is not because the government awarded those positions to African Americans. It's because, given opportunity by the Voting Rights Act of 1965, millions of Black southerners—even after that act still at the risk of violence and death—organized themselves, walked past the voting booth curtain, and marked their ballots for people they believed and hoped would truly represent them, their issues, their communities, their hopes and dreams.

Dreams and hopes were precisely what the term "freedom" suggested. The word itself is visionary, emotional, expansive, joyous: Freedom! To southern whites, it suggested that the African Americans they had kept down so long had something more in mind than a set of constitutional guarantees.

They were right.

One of the great traditional songs that helped lift spirits during the Southern Civil Rights Movement begins:

> They say that freedom is a constant struggle
> Oh, Lord, we've struggled so long
> We must be free, we must be free

In the summer of 1965, no one knew that better than the Black citizens of Forrest City, Arkansas.

~~~

One of the things that unsettled me most when I went South was the unbelievably raw racist language local whites used in daily conversation, in front of African Americans as well as, presumably, among themselves (understandably, I wasn't invited to all-white local gatherings). I don't believe in repeating hate speech, so I won't use the terms they did. But you know what I'm talking about.

I had been raised to challenge such words and phrases any time they came up. Back when I was in the third or fourth grade, a new student arrived from North Carolina, with a word I'd never heard before. I asked Mom what it was.

"It's a terrible word that some people in the South use to refer to Negroes," she said. "No one should ever use it."

This was in the early 1950s, before "Black" and "African American" came into common use. "Negro" was then considered the most respectful of the various terms available.

That wasn't the word the new arrival was throwing around the schoolyard.

"Well, he's sure using it," I responded.

"You go back tomorrow and tell him he's not in North Carolina any more. He's in Pennsylvania now. He can't talk like that up here."

I was not particularly excited at the prospect of confronting my new classmate. "Mom," I stalled, "this is a pretty big kid. If I tell him that, he's likely to beat me up."

"I'll fix you up," Mom said. "I always do, don't I?"

I honestly don't remember what happened the next day—whether I said anything or not, what I told Mom when I got home. But I have never forgotten what she said to me.

Still, it's not always easy to know when to challenge someone, when to take on the language, the jokes, the stereotypes. It's one thing in your personal life, where it's really up to you and your conscience how to deal with friends and relatives who step over that particular line. When you're working as an organizer, your actions have implications that go beyond the personal.

I was once lucky enough to be in an audience of young activists listening to a talk by Wiley Branton, a leading Black civil rights lawyer, originally from Arkansas. Branton told us a story that illustrates the complexity of such situations—and the extent to which they involve ethical as well as practical considerations.

Branton had worked out a pretrial agreement with a white judge to dismiss the case against his African American client. When the case was called, to Branton's horror, the judge, instead of throwing the charges out of court as he'd promised to do, started to try the case.

Branton jumped to his feet. "Your honor," he said, "excuse me, but this is the case we spoke about previously."

The judge looked at Branton—puzzled at first, then nodding as he remembered the agreement.

"This is *your* n_____, Wiley?" he virtually shouted (in the South at that time, whites never addressed African Americans, even prominent attorneys, by their last names or with titles such as Ms., Mrs., or Mr., only by their first names). "Get your n_____ out of my courtroom."

Branton paused in his story and took a moment for the shock to sink in. He swung his gaze around the room, looking each of us in the eyes.

"So if you had been me," he asked us, "what would you have done? "Would you have said to the judge, 'Your honor, that word has no place in an American courtroom.' Or would you have moved as fast as you could, and gotten your client out of that judge's sight?"

I would add: If, in that situation, you were a white rather than a Black attorney, would the dynamics be different? Would you have the same set of responsibilities?

Whoever you are: What would you have done?

~~~

There's a saying that in the North white people don't care how high Black people get, as long as they don't get too close.

In the South, the saying continues, white people don't care how close Black people get, as long as they don't get too high.

I was about to discover that there is sometimes more truth to all this folk wisdom than I would have imagined.

If I was often shocked and angered by the racial dynamics in Forrest City and St. Francis County, I was sometimes pleasantly surprised. At one point, the SNCC leadership decided that to reinforce the Movement in the rural areas of the county we needed to help African American farmers start their own cooperative.

One afternoon, I was out in the country visiting with Ed Williams, one of the Black farmers working to organize the co-op. We were sitting in the family's small but spotless living room, no small achievement in a house that was barely able to keep itself from falling over in a light breeze. The requisite shotgun leaned against the wall by the front door; a hot breeze blew through the open window.

Suddenly, the front door opened, and a very large white man wearing overalls and brogans—lace-up leather work boots—walked in. I thought my time had come.

He turned to the Black farmer. "Ed, do you mind?" he asked.

Ed shrugged. "You know where they are. Bring me one, too. And one for him." He pointed in my direction.

The gigantic white man disappeared into the kitchen. I heard the refrigerator door open and, a second later, slam shut.

He was back in a heartbeat—mine—with three beers. He handed one to Ed and one to me, settled himself comfortably in the only empty chair, popped the lid, and took a long swallow.

By the time he lowered the beer can, he and Ed were both laughing. There was no doubt they were laughing at me. I must have looked terrified—not surprising, given that I was.

"It's okay," Ed said. "We're neighbors."

It had never occurred to me that such a thing as I was seeing was possible—not in St. Francis County, Arkansas, in the summer of 1965.

"It's like this," the white farmer said. "Out here in the country, we've got to get along. If my log chain breaks, I'm not going to run my tractor a mile up the road to find some white farmer who's got one, when Ed's got the next farm up from me. I'm coming up here to Ed's place, and I'm going to borrow his log chain." He grinned. "And, of course," lifting the can, "one or two of his beers."

He took another long swallow. "If the white folks in Forrest City knew how we live out here in the country, they'd come out here and kill us all, Black and white."

~~~

I've also learned that no matter how many years you've been doing creative community organizing you're never quite as smart as you think you are. Unfortunately, when I was with SNCC in Arkansas, I hadn't figured that out yet. If it hadn't been for the wisdom and experience of older hands, that attitude could have landed me in what in the South we call "a mess of trouble."

I wasn't looking for trouble that particular day, just piloting my '53 Chevy down one of the dirt streets on the Black side of Forrest City. I was paying very careful attention to the speed limit.

If you were a SNCC worker, one mile per hour over that line, and the strong arm of the law was likely to whip out and snatch you.

So I didn't understand it when Sergeant Jim Wilson pulled his squad car alongside and motioned to me to pull over.

"Let's see your wallet," he said, leaning against my car like it was his personal property. I handed it over. He shuffled casually through it.

"Was I going too fast, Officer?" I asked as politely as I could. I knew I hadn't been, but it was going to be his word against mine. I figured I might as well find out where matters stood.

"Nope. You were under the speed limit."

Well, that was a relief. "So is it all right if I keep going?"

"Nope." He wasn't in a particularly conversational mood.

"There's a problem?"

"You've got Maryland plates and a Maryland driver's license. You've been in Arkansas more than thirty days. That means you're supposed to have Arkansas plates and an Arkansas driver's license."

I know that the truth is always the best defense, but in this case it wasn't going to help. I'd been in the state just a shade over thirty days, and I knew it.

Sometimes a creative community organizer can be a little too creative. I decided to lie.

"No, sir," I said, "It's close to thirty, but it's not thirty yet."

"Follow me," he said. I did.

At the police station, we each presented our case. By now, I had decided to pin down my arrival in Arkansas to a date exactly twenty-nine days previous. The magistrate seemed sympathetic. "He says he got here twenty-nine days ago," he told the officer. "He seems pretty sure of it."

"Then how come he got an Arkansas fishing license thirty-two days ago?" The officer held up the damning evidence as if it were the severed head of an enemy warrior.

Ouch. I had forgotten about that.

It's the only time in my life I've been undone by my love of fishing.

That's how I ended up in the Forrest City jail. Other SNCC workers had gone to jail for sitting in at white-only lunch counters, violating restraining orders, picketing without a permit, refusing to move when ordered to do so by the police or sheriff.

I was in jail for having an Arkansas fishing license.

At first I was in a holding cell. There was a little barred window on one side of it. Pretty soon a face appeared there.

"Hey," the face said.

"Hey," I answered.

"I'm a civil rights worker," the face said. "They've had me locked up here for two months."

It was the first time I'd seen a civil rights worker with a military-style haircut. His gray sweatshirt looked like it had just come from the laundry. I decided I'd better be a little bit careful.

"You're a civil rights worker, too, aren't you?" the face asked.

I knew that information wasn't on my fishing license, so there was no way to prove it one way or the other. "Nope, just passing through," I said. It was clearly my day to lie.

"Do you know Daisy Bates?" the voice asked. She was one of the heroes of the Movement in Arkansas, the longtime president of the state NAACP.

"I don't believe so," I said. This time my answer was true. I would have been honored to meet her, but in fact never had. "Does she live here?"

The face disappeared from the window and reappeared at the cell door. The gray sweatshirt was gone, replaced by the police uniform that had undoubtedly been under it all along.

"You've got a visitor," he said.

One of the local leaders was waiting for me. Word had gotten back to the Freedom Center that I was in jail. "Hang on," he said. "We're putting your bail money together as fast as we can. We're going to get you out of here. Don't you worry."

If I had to choose one moment in my forty-five years as an organizer to illustrate how fundamentally smart I really am, what follows would not be the one.

"No, don't do that," I said. "Leave me in here, at least overnight. It's just what we need to get people fired up. Think of the mass meeting we can have tomorrow."

He looked at me like I was crazy. He was right.

"Uh-huh," he said, with that particular southern inflection that compresses several paragraphs into five letters, and walked out.

My new friend from the police department escorted me back upstairs to the white "tank"—the jail, like everything else in Forrest City, was segregated. Inside were three white men who looked like deserters from the Confederate Army.

"Here's a civil rights worker for you, boys," my host said. "You can do whatever you want with him." He opened the door and shoved me in.

There was a long, long pause, in which we all cautiously eyed each other. Finally, one of the battle-weary Confederates spoke. "Are you really a civil rights worker?"

His New Jersey accent shimmered like an oasis in the desert. Perhaps there was hope after all.

"I am." My brief romance with lying was apparently over.

"Do you know Martin Luther King?"

"I don't."

"Do you know anybody who knows him?"

I thought hard. "I might."

"You think you could get a message to them?"

"Might could." Inspired by Sergeant Wilson, I was getting good at two-syllable responses.

"Well, you see if you can't get a message to Martin Luther King. You tell him to bring his people over here and march them around this sorry-ass jail until they let us out."

One of the other shadows spoke. "These sons of bitches done violated our civil rights."

"Locked me up for drunk driving, when I hadn't had more than three beers in two hours." The first speaker was clearly the captain commanding these ragged troops. "That's a civil rights violation right there. Isn't that right, Joe."

It was a statement, not a question. Obediently, the third prisoner spoke up.

"That's right, Sam. Plus keeping us in this hole for two months without bail. Don't forget that."

Captain Sam turned to me. "You tell all that to Martin Luther King, now." It was a command, clear as day.

I was trying to figure out just how I was going to carry out the order when I heard the cell door open. Sure enough, it was my crew-cutted acquaintance from the holding cell.

"You just got bailed out," he said.

I followed him down the stairs. The local leader was waiting for me, smiling.

I have rarely been so grateful to anyone for ignoring my advice.

Crew cut handed me back my wallet and car keys. I had just started out the door when I heard him say, "Wait a minute."

I stopped and turned around. He was holding out my fishing license.

"Better take this," he said. "You never know when you might need it."

～～～

I don't want to overestimate these moments, or the many others like them I've seen over the years. But I also don't want to underestimate them. As an organizer, I live and work in hope. To keep going, day after day, year after year, I need to have faith, to believe that human beings, no matter how much they may hate each other, can somewhere find some common connection, some thread, some knot, some glimmer of recognition. I have to believe they can take that as a starting point and slowly, painfully, over time, make their way towards each other. To do that, I have to suspend my own disbelief, to learn to check my stereotypes at the door.

Every once in a while I go downtown at night in Charlotte, North Carolina, where I've lived for the past thirty years, and get an outside table at one of my favorite restaurants, Mert's, a sort of nouvelle soul food place where you can get vegetarian collard greens and eat to the sound of sweet southern gutbucket blues. It's right across the street from Cosmos, a nightclub that caters to the late teens/early twenties set. The young people standing outside, talking animatedly to each other, smiling and laughing, are a wonderful mix of human types—so many shades, shapes, sizes, facial characteristics, languages, accents. Across lines of race and ethnicity, they hold hands, embrace, kiss.

I sit there in the relative dark, under the restaurant canopy. I think: This is part of what I've worked for all these years, that a young Black man and a young white woman can laugh together on a warm summer night in Charlotte, North Carolina, and no one will even notice.

I go on: If this were forty-five years ago, and young people of different races were standing like this anywhere in the South, laughing together as they are tonight, the Klan would be out in force, screaming viciousness at them, brandishing baseball bats and two-by-fours. The police would screech to a halt in their cruisers, perhaps to keep the Klan away from the terrified kids, perhaps to join in. Parents would arrive in a panic to drag their children home. White daughters and sons would be sent to live with relatives in other cities, to boarding schools and military academies. Black parents would be fired and evicted.

Tonight, there is none of that, just the sounds of young people looking for love.

Never accept the stereotypes that frighten and freeze us into inaction—even when they're your own.

Never, never stop believing that change is possible.

Don't Just Study History—Make It

On the southeast corner of Greene Street and Waverly
On the east side of Washington Square
The street is still troubled, the sidewalk unsettled
Young voices still cry through the afternoon air
March 25th, 1911
This is the way she told it to me
A factory of immigrants, Jews and Italians
Are hard at their work when the fire breaks free

> At the Triangle Shirtwaist Factory
> Women fall through the bitter spring air
> Their young faces turn to question me
> I still hear their voices
> As I walk through Washington Square

They rush for the doors, but the bosses have locked them
Lest someone step out for a breath of fresh air
Trapped in this wreckage, they run to the windows
Stare ten stories down to the street lying there
They stand on the ledges, the fire behind them
The wide air before them, they jump holding hands
They cry out in Yiddish, cry out in Italian
And plunge to the street where my own mother stands

Thirty years later, she still can't believe it
She cries through her story, I sit at her feet
One hundred twenty three immigrant women
Twenty-three men lie dead in the street
This is our history, this moment that shapes us
My mother falls silent, tears frame her cheeks
She could never forget, I will always remember
It could have been her, it still could be me

*E*very once in a while, someone asks me, "So what did you study in college to prepare yourself to become an organizer?"

I'm sure I could name a number of fields that would cause the questioner to nod sagely and say, "Of course. I thought so." I'm not absolutely sure what all those fields are, but I suspect economics, sociology, African American/ LGBTQ/Native American/ women's/U.S. history, political science, or even statistics would all earn that coveted nod of approval.

My undergraduate degree is in medieval history and literature.

"Medieval history and literature," they repeat, trying hard not to make the sentence end with a combination question mark and exclamation point, to look impressed and fascinated rather than puzzled and disappointed.

Usually I just smile and let it go. But, if they're persistent, I say, "It turns out that if you're going to spend your life trying to organize the South, a working knowledge of feudalism is a very good thing to have."

As it happens, I didn't study medieval history and literature because I had decided on an organizing career and thought this was the best possible preparation. At that time in my life, I didn't even know there was such a thing as an organizer. I chose to study it because I loved it.

I was particularly fascinated by the troubadours of the twelfth and thirteenth centuries. With some notable exceptions, such as the wealthy and powerful William IX, twelfth-century ruler of the Kingdom of Aquitaine in what is now southern France, the troubadours were impoverished poet/musicians (they sang rather than recited their lyrics). They wandered the European countryside, picking up work and a handful of coins wherever they could, depending on the kindness and hospitality of friends and strangers for food, drink, and a bed for the night.

At some subliminal level, I must have known even then that I was going to become not only a community organizer, but a folksinger.

So my professional training is as a historian. But my mantra is not, "Those who fail to study history are doomed to repeat it." One thing I've learned by studying history is how rare it is to find agreement even on what happened, let alone what whatever happened actually means.

It follows that I don't believe whatever lessons we can derive from history are particularly useful or accurate in predicting or trying to shape the future. It's kind of like the Devil quoting scripture: Take any historical event or period, and you can use it to prove or predict pretty much anything you want to.

More importantly, I don't think we're doomed to repeat anything. I absolutely refuse to believe or accept that. Rather, I believe that, by the work human beings do, individually and collectively, we create our future—for better or worse.

What I believe history does teach us is that in the broad struggle for justice you never really know what's possible and what's not. So, as creative community organizers, we need to be very careful not to limit the hopes and dreams of the people we work with. If we are not careful, our hardheaded "realism," historical "knowledge," and strategic "sensibility" may hold people back from taking on apparently unwinnable fights—that, if they are wise enough to ignore our advice, may instead turn out to be critical, deeply significant victories.

Here's one way this potential problem plays out. One of the first things you learn when you're trained as a community organizer is the "stop sign principle." Let's say you've just started working in an inner-city neighborhood where several children have been hurt recently in a busy intersection with no stop sign. The people you're talking with feel powerless and isolated. Insofar as their current status relative to the people and institutions that control the city, they're not wrong.

But they do have dreams: Of city government that works for them, not against them. Of neighborhood schools that give their children both a real education and a fair chance at work and life. Of safety and security at home, at work, and on the streets. Of secure jobs with a living wage, solid benefits, and safe working conditions.

The problem, given the realities of power in the city, is that there's very little chance that they will get any of these things any time in the foreseeable future. If they go after them and are soundly defeated, they'll end up feeling even more powerless and discouraged than before.

So, as an organizer working in that community, you look for a "fixed fight" as a first effort—a campaign that would be almost impossible to lose.

While you and the people you're working with try to figure out what to do, yet another truck speeds through the intersection. Moving too quickly, the driver doesn't even see the neighborhood kid crossing the street.

The people in the community are grief stricken and outraged. How could "they" let this happen? This isn't the first time a child has been hurt or killed on that corner. The city knew how dangerous the intersection was. It wouldn't have cost them much of anything, in time or in money, to put up a stop sign.

If this had happened in a wealthy neighborhood, a white neighborhood, a middle-class neighborhood, the city would have been out there in an hour. But they've never paid attention to poor folks, to working folks, to immigrants, to people of color, to people like *us*. This time, we're going to make sure that they do.

Under these emotional circumstances, it's relatively easy to get people to come to a meeting, pass around petitions, go as a group to see the mayor, pack the city council meeting, and demand—not suggest—that the city immediately put up a stop sign on that corner.

Even a not very smart mayor is going to send out the street crew, if not first thing in the morning, then very soon. What do they have to lose? The city has a warehouse full of stop signs. The street crew is already on the municipal payroll, and it's an hour's work at best.

If the city doesn't act, and another child gets hurt or killed at the same intersection, the mayor and city council members could be in real trouble, come the next election. It doesn't take much for what started out as a fight over a neighborhood stop sign to escalate into a citywide racial issue, with electoral consequences.

So, from the mayor's point of view: On the one hand, a relatively easy, pretty much cost-free fix, with some possible gratitude and votes from the people in the neighborhood—not enough to swing or sway an election, but, when you're running for office, every vote really does count. On the other hand, a potentially embarrassing situation, with the wrong kind of media attention and the possibility of discontent spreading to other neighborhoods and groups in the city.

The stop sign goes up. Sure enough, people in the neighborhood are going to feel a new sense of pride, power, and possibility.

The stop sign principle is a useful community tool. But in any urban, suburban, or rural area today, with the limited financial resources available to local governments, you run out of fixed fights pretty quickly. It's one thing to put up a stop sign: no real cost, no serious political risk. Other neighborhoods aren't going to complain if the first one gets a stop sign at a corner where a child has been hurt or killed.

But as the stakes get higher, the fixes get harder. Now the neighborhood, empowered by its victory, wants a community center, a job training program, a public library, a publicly funded facility that creates jobs for local people.

Well, so do thirty-four other neighborhoods, and they're going to fight for what they want. The pie gets a lot harder to slice. Your neighborhood keeps fighting, too, but now they're losing instead of winning—again and again. The city is only going to build one new bus maintenance depot. One neighborhood is going to get the facility and the jobs that go with it—and thirty-four aren't.

Over time, the pride, the sense of power and possibility, begin to slip away.

This doesn't have to happen. The neighborhood can reach out to others and help organize a citywide neighborhood coalition that eventually builds enough collective power to push through policy changes that work for everyone.

But the danger in the stop sign principle is always there. That doesn't mean it shouldn't be applied, just that every community organizer needs to be aware of how complex, and how potentially risky in the long run, this apparently simple strategy really is.

Another problem with the stop sign principle relates to an insight that organizers can learn from history.

On the one hand, it's true that when people get an early victory they begin to understand and believe in organizing as a way to make their lives better, individually and collectively.

On the other, one of the things that makes human beings so remarkable and wonderful is our capacity for visionary imagination, the ability to believe that something can happen when common sense says there is absolutely no way. Another amazing characteristic is our radical tenacity, the ability to fight for decades for something that is truly important to us, even when everyone around us is sure that what we so fervently wish and fight for will never come to pass.

The Southern Civil Rights Movement is an example of such a fight. As someone who came of age politically in that movement, I have great gratitude for it. It not only showed me what I needed to do with my life, it taught me who I really am. I had not in any true sense known that before. If not for the Movement, I might not know it today.

So as what was once daily life for me becomes history, I read as much about that period as I can. One of my favorite books is *There Is a River*, by the African American theologian Vincent Harding.

Harding describes the movement for Black liberation as a current that never stops flowing. Sometimes its path is as visible as the course of the Mississippi River, seen from thirty thousand feet up on a clear day. Sometimes it overflows its banks as a mighty flood, moving everything in its path. Sometimes the river runs underground, and people wonder where it's gone.

But the river is always there. It overflowed into history on February 1, 1960, when four young African American students from Greensboro A&T, a historically Black college (now university) in North Carolina, sat down at a whites-only Woolworth's lunch counter, ordered coffee, and refused to leave when ordered to do so.

The springs that fed that river began flowing in 1619, when the first Africans captured and transported by Arab and European traders are shoved off the boat and dumped into the slave market in Jamestown, Virginia.

Follow carefully, now. See the river run through slave revolts led by Nat Turner, Denmark Vesey, and a hundred others. Walk along its banks with Harriet Tubman and the other angry conductors on the Underground Railroad, following the North Star toward freedom. Look on in admiration as former slave Frederick Douglass sets by hand the type on his Abolitionist newspaper *The North Star*. Watch as white Abolitionist women go door-to-door in their villages and along country roads, carrying petitions demanding that slavery end.

They are all there, following the river road. The Black veterans returning from World Wars I and II, who, having fought to defend the freedom of a country that will not allow them to be free, decide it's time for a change. Ella Baker, organizing for the

NAACP in Alabama in the early 1940s, when it was an illegal organization in that state, and you could be sent to prison for being caught with a membership card. Dedicated white Communist Party members, like Saul and Isabelle Auerbach, who go South under false names to help organize a Black national liberation movement within the states of the old Confederacy.

The Little Rock Nine, courageous young African American high school students, clutching their school books close to their chests, walking in carefully ironed dresses, pants, and shirts past rows of grim-faced white Arkansas National Guardsmen towards the entrance of Central High School in Little Rock in 1957 as furious white parents threaten and spit at them.

I imagine them, and I remember.

> Late in the evening as light fades away
> In silence we gather together
> Searching the faces of those who are here
> For those who have left us forever

Waiting for them, literally standing in the schoolhouse door to block their way, is Governor Orval Faubus. A graduate of Commonwealth College, a socialist school in Mena, Arkansas, he lost his first electoral race because he ran as a racial moderate, and he promised himself that would never, never happen to him again as long as he lived. Looking out at the crowds of angry whites, held back only by the guardsmen with their bayonets from overwhelming these Black students, who are only a few years younger than the soldiers, the governor is doing his best to keep his promise.

I stay up late at night, sometimes until dawn, reading about these brave, determined warriors. I wonder at their courage, their grace, their stubbornness over more than three centuries. I recall the brave students of Greensboro, of their nonviolent shot that was truly heard 'round the world, and I say to myself: This moment was destined to happen, almost exactly when and as it did.

When you read the wonderful historians who have documented and analyzed the many events that led to the Southern Civil Rights Movement, what becomes clear is that movement's inevitability. But at the time only a few people believed the visionaries of the 1940s and 1950s, whose predictions went something like this: "In the early 1960s, young southern African Americans, supported by their allies of many other races all over the world, will rise up by the thousands. They will deliberately break segregation's unjust laws. Every possible lie will be told about them. But still they will stand up, they will sit down, they will sit in. They will throw their bodies against the wall dividing Black from white; they will take their bare hands and tear it down. They will be beaten; they will cry out. They will go to jail; offered bail, they will refuse. They will be beaten, murdered and lynched."

> Where are the ones who caught flame in the night
> Fired up by the heat of devotion
> Measuring their lives by the light of the truth
> They burned like a lamp on the ocean

No one really knew for sure that it was coming, yet it had to come. When you consider how heavily the deck was stacked against them, that moment should never have arrived; and yet it came. The odds against them were so long that they should have gone down to defeat; and yet they won.

> Who will remember the words of the brave
> That lifted us higher and higher
> Who will remember the price that they paid
> For lives lived too close to the fire

There were people in the 1950s who had another vision: "The day will come when the doors of Robben Island Prison swing wide, to let Nelson Mandela and the leaders of the African National Congress walk out into the fresh air of freedom. Apartheid will fall. Mandela will be elected president of South Africa."

Many people would have replied, "That's crazy. Mandela and his friends will rot in prison before the white South African government ever lets them out. Apartheid is too deeply entrenched, too strongly defended, to ever be brought down. You need to get real. Organizing for things that will never happen only makes things worse. An end to apartheid, freedom for the ANC leadership, a racially integrated government—better stop dreaming. Let's focus instead on eliminating the worst sins of apartheid, on making it a more humane, more manageable system. That might be within our reach."

As organizers, part of our responsibility is never to forget this history lesson: You never know what is possible. We can never truly predict what human beings working together can accomplish—and therefore we can never compromise with injustice.

Yes, we should study history. But, as organizers, we should also help people make history.

> Hearts of the ones who inherit your lives
> Will rest in the truth you have spoken
> Memory will echo the trust that you kept
> Like you, it will never be broken

As creative community organizers, our job is to help people learn not just history, but also how to carry it on. If we fail to remember our roots, if we forget the lessons of the past, if we don't remember and honor so many astounding victories won against unbelievable odds, we limit the possibilities of the future.

Whatever else, we must always be careful not to stand between the people we work with and their impossible dreams.

Recognize Risks

The air is thick as silence, you can cut it with a knife
A man lies in the hospital, draining out his life
The trucks are on the back roads
In the dark their headlights shine
There's one man dead on the Harlan County line

Anger like a poison is eating at your soul
Your thoughts are loud as gunfire, your face is hard as coal
Bitterness like buckshot explodes inside your mind
There's one man dead on the Harlan County line

A miner's life is fragile, it can shatter just like ice
But those who bear the struggle
Have always paid the price
There's blood upon the contract, like vinegar in wine
There's one man dead on the Harlan County line

From the river bridge at High Splint
To the Brookside railroad track
You can feel a long strength building
That can never be turned back
The dead go forward with us, not one is left behind
There's one man dead on the Harlan County line

The night is cold as iron, you can feel it in your bones
It settles like a shroud upon
The grave of Lawrence Jones
The graveyard shift is walking
From the bathhouse to the mine
There's one man dead on the Harlan County line

*S*ometime during the late summer of 1973, I stopped off in Pittsburgh, where the United Mine Workers of America were holding their annual convention. My first cousin was on the UMWA staff. I went up to his hotel room to visit for a while.

He was lying on the bed, a wet washcloth covering his eyes, moaning softly.

"What's the matter?" I asked. "Are you all right?"

He lifted the washcloth and looked at me like I was crazy. "No, I'm not all right. If I was all right, do you think I'd be lying in the bed with a cold washcloth over my head?" He looked like he was going to pass out on the spot. "I've got this splitting headache," he added unnecessarily.

I had figured that out. "Are you sick? Do I need to get you a doctor?"

"It's not that." He shook his head painfully. "It's this strike we've got in Harlan County." He paused. "There's something I need you to do."

Now, to most people, the words "Harlan County" conjure up something from the old TV sitcom *The Dukes of Hazzard*—the real town of Hazard, which is in Perry County, being just a stone's throw from the town of Harlan, in Harlan County. Maybe, if they're country music fans from the old days, they might know the song *Nine Pound Hammer*, first recorded commercially by The Hillbillies in 1927:

> It's a long way to Harlan
> It's a long way to Hazard
> Just to get a little brew, boys
> Just to get a little brew
> Now roll on buddy
> Don't you roll so slow
> How can I roll, roll, roll
> When the wheels won't go

But for anyone who knows the Appalachian coalfields, who knows the mountains, who knows coal mining and the UMWA, what comes immediately to mind is the phrase "Bloody Harlan," bestowed on the county in the 1930s, when strikes were settled by rifles, pistols, and dynamite.

When you've got trouble in Harlan County, Kentucky, you've got real trouble.

Here's what caused my cousin's headache. In the 1930s, under the leadership of Welsh immigrant coal miner John L. Lewis, the UMWA was as powerful and successful as any union in the United States. But by the 1960s, its leadership had grown corrupt and lazy. Thousands of union members were disabled, dying from black lung disease, caused by breathing in coal dust every day. When technology gave the industry faster, more powerful machines to mine the coal, the dust grew finer and thicker. The miners got sicker and sicker, more and more quickly.

But the UMWA leadership, enjoying the good life in Washington, D.C., far from the coalfields, didn't care and weren't there. They abandoned their own loyal members, who were spitting up sputum black with coal dust, sleeping upright in armchairs so as not to smother from the weight of their own lungs, coughing themselves and their families awake every night, living on bottled oxygen and borrowed time. These miners may not have known all the medical ins and outs of what was happening to them. But they did know something was deeply wrong, with them and with the system.

More than that, they knew how to organize, how to fight for what they knew was theirs by right. In the old days when the UMWA was being built, what they fought for were higher wages, better working conditions, vacations, pensions, and "portal-to-portal" pay.

Now it was hospital cards, medical care, and compensation so that while they were still barely hanging on to life they'd have at least a little something coming in to support their wives and children, and then to help keep their loved ones going after they'd passed on.

In the 1930s and 1940s, the UMWA was in the forefront of the struggle for justice, fighting with a sense of hope and possibility:

> I'm tired of working for nothing
> And bad top that's ready to fall
> If we can't dig this coal without danger
> We ain't gonna dig it at all

>> And the wind blows hard up the holler
>> Through the trees with a whistling sound
>> But the sun's gonna shine in this old mine
>> Ain't no one can turn us around

A lot had changed since the old days. The UMWA leadership should have been leading the fight for safety in the mines and for compensation for those disabled by working conditions underground, as well as for the widows and orphans of those who died from black lung. But they were nowhere to be seen.

So, in this desperate situation, in which those who should have been responsible and responsive just plain weren't, people throughout the coal camps and former company towns throughout the southern mountains turned to creative community organizing. Starting in West Virginia and eventually spreading throughout the Appalachian coalfields, they stood up and fought back together as the Black Lung Association. Former miners broken down so badly by black lung they could barely stand, widows and orphans of those who had been choked to death by dust from the coal they spent their lives digging, were backed up by their kinfolk, neighbors, rank and file members of the UMWA who were still working, members of other unions, small-business owners, local elected officials, and clergy.

In the coalfields in those days, it seemed like just about everybody who was working in the mines, or who had ever worked in them, was kin to half the county. Sometimes they really were. In these communities, knit tightly by danger and disaster, the old labor motto "An injury to one is an injury to all" was not just history. It was daily life.

What the people of the Black Lung Association did, the strategies and tactics they used to make black lung not just a coalfield but a national issue, how they eventually won a federal black lung benefits program—that's a history in itself. For the purpose of understanding creative community organizing, what's important is that in the face of unresponsiveness from the organization that should have represented and fought for them, the UMWA, they built an alternative organization to do what the UMWA should have done in the first place.

That's one of the core principles of creative community organizing: When an institution that has a responsibility to everyday people fails to do its job, one option is to build another organization to challenge the first one and force it to do the right thing. That principle holds whether the institution being challenged is a union, a corporation, a unit of government—whether tribal, territorial, city, county, state, or federal—or an educational or religious institution.

The other option is not only to build an alternative organization, but then to use it as a base to take over the original one.

That's just what the people of the Appalachian coalfields did. While the Black Lung Association was organized and led primarily by disabled miners and their families, with support from those who were still working underground, Miners for Democracy was organized and led by working members of the UMWA, with support from members of the Black Lung Association.

The goal of Miners for Democracy was no less than to take over the union that had turned its back on the miners. Eventually, the working miners who led the organization in its fight for union reform—many of whom had also been active in the Black Lung Association—were elected as the new leadership of the UMWA, and they moved into the stately union headquarters in the heart of the nation's capital.

So this was the United Mine Workers of America in 1973, when in response to my cousin's request I started working on the Brookside Strike. The UMWA was unusual within the labor movement of that time in that the leadership knew how to apply a creative community organizing approach to union organizing.

As soon as I arrived in Brookside, Kentucky, I noticed that just about everyone in the small community was pitching in to help the striking miners and their families. Local bluegrass bands played at every rally and mass meeting. Even if they didn't know any of the old labor anthems like *Solidarity Forever* or *Roll the Union On*, their presence was strong statement enough.

On a Saturday morning, if you drove down the main highway through what passed for a town, past the entrance to the Brookside mine and the picket line that ran twenty-four hours a day to keep the mine closed, women holding plastic milk jugs stepped directly in front of your vehicle and asked for a contribution to help feed the families of those on strike. If some of that money went to buy ammunition instead of milk, no outsider was the wiser.

When pro-company judges issued restraining orders to keep the striking miners away from the picket line, these same women took over, with a fierceness and determination that was both awe inspiring and, for any strikebreaker, or "scab," attempting to cross the line, terrifying. The women used iron pipes to bust out the windshields of the cars and trucks the scabs were driving, dragged them out through the broken glass, and chased them down the road, raining blows on them at every opportunity.

The mines stayed closed.

～～～

One of the challenges in creative community organizing is knowing when a local fight has to be moved to the next level. If the picket line that kept the Brookside mine closed had been broken, if non-union miners had been able to cross the line in large enough numbers to get the mines working again, the strike would have been lost.

But even if they could keep the mines in Harlan County closed forever, the Brookside miners wouldn't win a union contract. Those mines accounted for a small percentage of the coal used by Carolina-based Duke Power Company, which had recently bought up the properties of the family-owned Eastover Mining Company, including the Brookside mine. Duke could get as much coal as they wanted through long-term contracts and from the spot market, buying it as they needed it. As far as Duke Power was concerned, their mines in Harlan County could stay closed forever.

The next step, we agreed, was to carry the fight to Duke's home territory and build a set of organizations there to bring pressure on the company in their own backyard.

My cousin and I had a major fight about how to do it. "What we're going to do," he said, "is buy full-page ads that say 'Fight Duke Power's Rate Increase' in every newspaper in the Duke service area."

"I thought this was supposed to be about helping the folks at Brookside."

"We'll have something in the ads that says, 'Support the Brookside Miners.' But that's not what people in North and South Carolina care about. Those are the two least-unionized states in the country. Most people there wouldn't know a union if they tripped over it, and they could care less. What they're mad about is that Duke is trying to raise their electric rates by 17 percent. That's what will get them to act, if anything will."

That's a persuasive argument, one that any organizer understands. Although there are some wonderful activists who do "solidarity work," standing with others to support a struggle in which they have no personal stake beyond their passionate belief in the possibility of justice, most people are motivated primarily by their own immediate self-interest.

"So they'll read an ad." I shook my head scornfully. "Then what?"

"We'll have a coupon that people can send to a post office box in Durham if they want to help. We'll come with some organizational name that sounds authentically local—'Carolina Action,' or something like that."

"That's not how you organize." I was mad now. "That's just smoke and mirrors. You need to go door-to-door. You've got to talk to people one-on-one. You think people are going to take time to fill out a coupon, stick it in an envelope, lick a stamp, and send it to some organization that doesn't even have a street address? They're not crazy, you know."

I was wrong by six thousand people.

"No hard feelings," my cousin said. "Anyway, now you've got six thousand names. You can organize them any way you want."

I started calling around the country, asking everyone I knew if they'd loan me one good organizer for thirty days. By now the Brookside Strike was getting pretty well known; a lot of people and organizations responded. Within a few weeks, we had at least a dozen organizers working across the Carolinas. Some of them took the six thousand coupons and sorted them into stacks by primary zip codes. The towns with the tallest stacks got organizers.

In Harlan County, in the Carolinas, all around the United States, the UMWA and its allies turned up the heat. Miners in helmets, safety lamps, and kneepads passed out leaflets on Wall Street. The press ate it up. Some of those same miners came to Charlotte, where I now live, and picketed the Duke Power Company's headquarters during Duke's annual meeting, to support the resolutions that shareholders all around the country had filed.

When you watch *Harlan County U.S.A.*, Barbara Kopple's Academy Award-winning documentary about the Brookside Strike, and you come to that scene, look to the right side of the screen. There I am, uncharacteristically wearing a suit and tie, keeping an eye on the picket line while I wait to go inside the shareholder meeting to challenge Duke Power's president, Carl Horn.

The pressure kept building. Something had to give—and it did. I was back home in the North Georgia mountains when I got the call. It was Barbara Kopple. "Lawrence Jones just got shot on the picket line," she said, half anger and half grief. "He's in the hospital. It doesn't look like he's going to make it."

～～

People become organizers because they want to help other people make their lives better. That's a good way to feel, and a fine thing to do.

But there's a built-in problem hardly anyone ever talks about. No matter how well we do our work, however conscientiously and carefully, even the best organizers occasionally make people's lives worse—sometimes for a while, sometimes forever.

Those we challenge—those who hold power over other people's lives—didn't get where they are by accident. They're not interested in losing the wealth and ease of life they enjoy. When they fight, they fight hard, and they fight to win.

When established power is challenged, people can get hurt, sometimes badly. They lose jobs, homes, cars. They're shunned, banned, blacklisted, run out of town. Their relationships suffer and break up. In some cases (less common in the United States today, at least compared to our past history, but quite the norm in some other countries), they're beaten, raped, imprisoned, tortured, murdered.

Here's the hard part. We as organizers bear at least some responsibility for what happens to the people we've encouraged to take these risks. It's easy to say, "It's the fault of those in power." But it is the organizer who says, "You don't need to take this any more. You need to stand up and speak out. You need to challenge injustice, for your own and your children's sake."

If people don't listen and don't do what organizers ask them to do, the conditions they want to challenge and change might continue for the rest of their lives—but they might not suffer the loss and pain they now have to live with.

I am hardly guilty of Lawrence Jones's murder. I am not the security guard who aimed the shotgun and pulled the trigger. I am not the company official who retained the security company. I am not the security company supervisor who employed the guard and gave him his instructions, whatever they were.

But I am also completely removed from the fact of Lawrence Jones's death.

What responsibility, then, do we as creative community organizers have when things go wrong? How do we learn to think about, act on, and live with these moral dilemmas?

I think about this question a lot. Every once in a while I ask myself: Suppose I could go back in time and sit down to a cup of something with each of the people I've tried to help organize over the past forty-five years. How many of them would be truly glad to see me, would sit across the table and thank me for being a part of what we'd done together back then?

Would any of them say, "You never should have showed up, Si. You should have left well enough alone. We were better off before you came."

And what would I do then?

Nearly thirty years after I left Forrest City, I went back for a visit, hoping to meet and talk with some of the amazing people from whom I'd learned so much. Not a one was left. Mervin Barr was long dead and buried. So now was Florence Clay, who had been the first to welcome the SNCC workers to town, who had let us sleep at the funeral home, whose son Jesse had occasionally gotten me to help out in the embalming room.

If there was still a Clay Funeral Home at all, I couldn't find it. The then almost-new brick building where I'd wandered at night among the open caskets was boarded up and overgrown. It reminded me of the great eastern Kentucky ballad maker Jean Ritchie's song about the coal camps that had been shut down and abandoned, with "kudzu vines growing up through the doorway."

The old wooden funeral home, which in the blistering heat of a Mississippi Delta summer we'd turned into the Forrest City Freedom Center, where I'd once found a set of false teeth in a dusty cupboard, was long gone, a weed-filled vacant lot in its place. On guard duty one night (we were nonviolent, we just wanted to be sure the white townspeople stayed nonviolent, too), sleeping on the floor facing the front door with a shotgun by my side, I once almost shot my SNCC coworker Dwight Simmons when he banged hard and loud on the front door at three in the morning. Waking up from a deep sleep, I thought the pounding on the door was the Klan trying to break in.

Long gone, too, was everybody I'd known, every last one of them. Jerry Casey, local leader of the SNCC project, who left town as soon as the Movement was over, just a step behind the Freedom Fighters returning to colleges, homes, and lives up North and out West. The Hicks brothers, Charles and Willie, with their smiles that could melt glass, with courage to match their grace and ease.

Those whose last and even first names I can't, at the distance of forty-five years, remember: Melvyn who worked at the lumber yard, who always managed to bring us just one more load of the materials we needed to build the Freedom Center, the tables where the local kids came to study the history they weren't taught in the Forrest City schools, the shelves for the little library to which people around the country sent books. Marie, who had been raped in the back of a police cruiser, who fed the SNCC workers just about every day in her little house across from the Freedom Center, with only the dusty track that passed for a road in the Black part of town between the two. Truman, who made it back from the Korean War to become the first African American to run for the Forrest City council, even though he lived out of town. The Black farmer who sold Truman a tiny sliver off the edge of the lot he owned inside the city limits, so Truman would be a city land-owner and eligible for public office. The white union president from the Yale and Townes forklift plant who came secretly to the Freedom Center under cover of darkness, asking for Black support in his race for mayor, as long as everyone kept their mouth shut so none of the other white folks would know what he'd done.

Had they left because they really wanted to, because it seemed so much brighter, so much more hopeful in Birmingham, Baltimore, Chicago, Cleveland, Detroit? Had it been made pain-fully clear to them that Forrest City, where they had been born and raised, gone to school and to work, married or not married, settled down or stayed stirred up, simply no longer had a place for them, now that the Movement had come and gone?

How many of them would tell me today that despite the hard-ship and suffering it was worth it after all?

So, as creative community organizers, what are we to do? What's our responsibility to those whose lives and communities we disrupt, however honorable our motives for intervening? How do we figure out when to encourage people, individually and collectively, to take risks—and when to discourage them from doing so?

To start with, we have to develop within ourselves and our organizations an ethics that helps us be both conscious and conscientious in all of our work. It's not wrong to ask people to risk their jobs, homes, reputations, even their lives.

What's wrong is to put people in situations where they take risks without fully knowing it. As ethical organizers, we need to be absolutely certain the people we work with truly recognize the risks they're taking, the things that could go wrong, the losses they might suffer, before they make the decision to act, individually or together.

For the most part, the communities where we organize are not our communities. The people we work with are not our families, our friends, our neighbors. When the organizing campaign is over, whether the battle is won or lost, whether the organization is built or not built, we leave. They stay.

So whatever decisions are made must be theirs, not ours. We have to refuse to push them into taking risks just because we might take them. The more sure we are of ourselves, of our experiences in other communities and campaigns, of our organizing skills, the more we have to struggle to avoid the arrogance of thinking we know what's right for other people. We need to recognize that when we raise the stakes they sometimes become much higher than we ever thought they would.

What we can and must offer—without promises, without assurances, without guarantees—is a clear choice between what has been, and what could be.

Lift Every Voice

I've been a trucker for most of my life
Can't tell you the places I've seen
I've pushed this old diesel from east coast to west
And about every place in between
The pleasures are many for a truck driving man
I've tasted them all in my time
But of all of my good times the one I like best
Is playing the old songs with old friends of mine

I left West Virginia to fight in the war
It's thirty-two years I've been gone
I wish I could stay here a few nights at least
But I've got to start driving at dawn
Making a living is hard work at best
But you know that it eases my mind
To know I can always stay here for the night
Playing the old songs with old friends of mine

John, take down your banjo from the nail on the wall
Jackie, come rosin that bow
Rich, hit us a lick on that sweet mandolin
We'll play every tune that we know

When the sun hits the mountain I'll be on my way
Got a long way to go down the line
As the miles slip by me I'll smile to think
Of playing the old songs with old friends of mine

I became an organizer because of how my parents raised me and because I was lucky to stumble into the Southern Civil Rights Movement when I was still young enough to have my working life shaped by it.

I became a songwriter because I fell in love with the old songs. I heard them first in the late 1950s on the old red vinyl LPs issued by the Library of Congress, later on Moe Asch's Folkways Records. The stark, spare recordings of Texas Gladden, Sin-Killer Griffin, Samantha Bumgardner, McKinley Morganfield (later to become famous as Muddy Waters), and Aunt Molly Jackson reached straight into my soul, rocked me, talked to me, reached me in ways that more apparently elaborate and acceptable musics had never been able to do.

In the 1960s and 1970s, working in the Deep South with SNCC and in the southern Appalachians with the UMWA, I discovered that not only were the old songs and people who wrote, rewrote, and sang them alive and well, but that many of these musicians were active in progressive movements, using their music as a tool for progressive change. I listened to the SNCC Freedom Singers (led by Bernice Johnson Reagon, later founder of Sweet Honey in the Rock), Sarah Ogan Gunning, Florence Reece, Dorothy Cotton, Nimrod Workman, Phyllis Boyens, George Pegram, Roscoe Holcomb, Hazel Dickens, and many others, not on a record player or concert stage, but on front porches, in living rooms, at rallies, in churches, and on picket lines. In African American churches, I heard choirs and congregations raise a joyful noise as together they sang James Weldon Johnson's great poem, set to music by his brother John Rosamond Johnson in 1900, known then as the Negro National Anthem:

> Lift every voice and sing
> 'Til earth and heaven ring
> Ring with the harmonies of Liberty;
> Let our rejoicing rise
> High as the listening skies,
> Let it resound loud as the rolling sea.
> Sing a song
> Full of the faith that the dark past has taught us,
> Sing a song
> Full of the hope that the present has brought us;
> Facing the rising sun of our new day begun,
> Let us march on 'til victory is won.

I was particularly impressed by the ability of these singers and songwriters to describe the lives of poor and working people, their hardships, heartaches, anger, pain, dreams, and struggles. In songs of apparent simplicity and directness, they conveyed rich layers of emotion and meaning. Their songs were often intensely political, but without the heavy-handedness of many so-called protest, struggle, and topical songs.

So I decided to write old songs as well as new ones, using the musical structures, rhythms, and cadences that were interwoven with the history of these time-honored movements for justice, of which I had now become a small part. These ancient poetic forms and structures—think of call and response songs as one example—serve a powerful purpose, bringing history forward, enriching the songs with memory.

New songs tend to describe. Old songs tell stories. Their language is conversational. In the best of them, you can hear the people who are living out the song's story talking to each other, just like they were sitting around the potbellied stove in some country store, chopping a long row of cotton, drinking corn whiskey in the shadows of the pines outside a country dance. The language is sparse, laconic, dry humored, economical. It's this understatement that allows the songs to be angry without moralizing, political without being preachy.

They do this partly by using as few words as possible. I had this lesson reinforced for me by the semi-legendary Dr. Banjo himself, Peter Wernick, Columbia sociology PhD turned bluegrass bandleader, whose brilliant production work and banjo playing helped bring the songs on my CD *Been a Long Time* to vibrant life. Successful bluegrass singing, Pete explained, depends on there being as few words in a song as possible, so that there's space for the singer to explore, emphasize, expand. He kept leaning on me to go through each song again and again, cutting every word that could possibly be cut, so that the remaining words would have enough space to breathe and do their job.

Many of the old songs are almost like paintings, parallels to the portraits and landscapes my mother Rosalind Kahn created in oils and watercolors. Even as we hear the song, whether we're singing along with others or just listening, we visualize it. We can see what's happening even as we hear the words.

You can say something in a song that you couldn't in ordinary speech, crank up a conversation you might otherwise have a hard time getting started. In a song called *Just a Lie*, I retell, with a slightly different cuisine, a story Pop once shared with me about his childhood. In winter, when evening came, his mother, my grandmother Celia Liebovitz Kahn, would send him and his three brothers out with sacks to walk the railroad track and pick up the coal that fell off the passing trains, so there would be fuel for the stove in the morning:

> Those good old days
> Were really low and mean
> With cornmeal mush
> And sometimes streak o'lean

> Picking up coal
> Along the railroad track
> Why would you want
> To have those hard times back

When my aunt Freda Shore was in her eighties, she remarried. She was the oldest of the five Kahn siblings, with the strenuous, thankless job of keeping the four roughhouse brothers in line.

At a celebratory supper at Pop's house after the ceremony, the seating was more or less by generations. I was out on the back porch with half a dozen of my first cousins. At one point, the conversation turned to trying to figure out what our family's class background was, and how to describe it accurately.

Pop, as the host for the evening, was making the rounds, checking in to make sure everyone was doing all right. As he passed our table, I called him over. Thinking about that story, I asked him whether he considered himself to have grown up poor.

I could see in his face how angry my question made him. "We were never poor." His voice was strained. "What ever gave you that idea?"

What about the story? I asked. Did he remember telling it to me? Was it even true?

"Oh, absolutely." Pop's stance shifted, his voice turned soft, his eyes warmed with memory. "Ma would send us out just about every evening in the fall and winter. Bill, Hoddy, Dubby, and me, we'd all go out together." I knew the brothers tended to stick close, at least partly to defend their late-night newspaper territory against the Irish kids who shared poverty with them. "We'd walk along the track and pick up coal until our sacks were full. Then we'd go home and give it to Ma, so she could build a fire in the morning and cook us all breakfast before she sent us off to school."

"Pop." I looked him as straight in the eyes as he would ever allow. "Scavenging for coal every night along the railroad tracks, so there's enough fuel to make a fire in the morning—you don't consider that growing up poor?"

"Absolutely not. We always had food on the table. Being poor means not having enough to eat."

Of course, since Pop grew up in an Orthodox Jewish household, there was never streak o'lean on his parents' table. A staple in poor southern households, both Black and white, it's bacon that's almost solid fat, with only the thinnest line of meat, or lean, passing through it.

~~~

Did you like the story?

Did it bring back something about your life, your family, memories fond or harsh?

Did it matter that perhaps you weren't raised Jewish, or poor, or religiously Orthodox, or in a mill town in New England with Yiddish-speaking parents who ran a tiny store in The Acre, for over a hundred years the traditional first stop for immigrants arriving in Lowell, Massachusetts? Or that you weren't one of four slightly crazy brothers who were sometimes just a little too quick with their tempers or fists?

Could you still find a place for yourself at the table, in the tale, around the coal-fired stove?

When creative community organizers use culture, we should make it as inclusive as possible. We need to tell stories from different cultures and traditions—including our own, but also many others. This means we tell them in a way that encourages and inspires the people with whom we work to tell their own stories, to share their own cultures.

Performance and presentation can be wonderful. Where would so many struggles for justice be without the many extraordinary artists who have made themselves a part of, and contributors to, those movements—and the organizers who have learned to use culture, quietly and effectively, in their work?

But, from the point of view of creative community organizing, participation is often, though not always, the thing to aim for.

We shouldn't be the only ones to tell stories. Everyone has them. Everyone needs to tell them.

Songs are for singing together, not just to perform for others. Choruses, especially short ones that repeat the same words and lines, and are therefore quickly learned, invite others into the song. That's why so many of the old songs, and the new songs that are modeled on them, repeat lines, couplets, choruses, over and over. That's one of the ways the old songs gather and build power.

> It's a long way to Harlan, long way to go
> Long way to Harlan, long way to home
> Yes it's a long way to Harlan, long way to go
> Long way to Harlan, long way to home

But it's not as long a way as you might think. The old songs do help take us home, even if they were written yesterday.

～～

By now, you will not be surprised to learn that I go through life humming to myself. On a clear day, you can hear me before you can see me. Even when by sheer mental effort I succeed in sealing my lips, if you look deep into my eyes, you can see the notes silently making their way along the staff.

Where did all this music come from? What is a nice Jewish boy doing singing in a place like this?

When I was growing up—not here in the South, where I've now lived and worked for forty-five years, but in the Deep North—our family sang together. On the Sabbath and on holidays, we would stay at the dinner table long after the food and dishes had been cleared, and we would sing. Because musical instruments were not allowed on the Sabbath, we sang without instrumentation—but not without accompaniment.

From my grandfather, Gabriel Kahn, who had traveled through Russia with his uncle's Yiddish-Italian opera troop, before he got drafted into the czar's army and suddenly became highly motivated to emigrate to the United States, I learned the fine points of creating a rhythm section, using only two basic variations (closed fist and open palm) of the basic hand-on-table technique. From my parents, Rosalind and Benjamin Kahn, I learned—once my sister Jenette Kahn and I had the basic tunes down—the rudiments of high and low harmony, made up as you go along.

The songs we sang were mostly prayers, composed thousands of years ago in Hebrew. There were prayers for different holidays, for the beginning of each lunar month, for the Sabbath, and for various combinations thereof.

Naturally, over that many years, melodies had changed. My mother's side of the family was convinced that my father's side had changed them, accidentally or deliberately, and vice versa. The preferred method for settling these disagreements was to sing as loudly as possible. Whichever side of the family was able to overwhelm the other was generally conceded to have history on its side, along with the correct version of the melody.

We sang a little bit in Yiddish, too, folk and story songs from the Old Country, which in this case meant almost any place in Europe. Hebrew had been the language of prayer for the Jews of Europe, but Yiddish was the language of everyday life. In our house, except for the songs, it had been reduced to the language of secrets, which our parents used when they wanted to communicate with each other privately in front of us. Despite this incentive to learn Yiddish, I never did, beyond the few phrases known to anyone who has lived in New York, regardless of race, color, creed, or national origin.

So the truth of the matter is that although I learned many songs and am amazed at how many I still know by heart, I never understood most of what I was singing. What's wonderful is that it never seemed to matter. I understood quite well what the songs really meant to us as Jews, as a family, as people in the world. They were our bond, our unity, our affirmation, our courage.

They were our way of claiming our rhythmic and harmonic relation with each other and with our community. Our songs reinforced our solidarity, our sense that we could overcome the obstacles in our path. They helped us feel proud of the side we were on.

~~~

This heritage came mostly from my father's side of the family. He was, after all, a rabbi, a teacher, someone who studied Talmud and *midrash*, the great collections of Jewish oral teaching and story-telling over many centuries. Pop was also religiously observant and deeply comfortable in that tradition.

My mother's upbringing had been as traditional and observant as my father's. But the branch of Judaism we now followed as a family was the conservative tradition (the term refers to religious observance and ritual, not to my parents' politics, which were quite progressive), which when I was growing up in the 1940s and 1950s reserved almost all of the public roles to men. Although I watched Mom light the candles on the Sabbath, I cannot remember her performing any other public or private religious ceremonies. (Contrary to folklore, cooking Jewishly is not a religious practice, nor is there anything in the tradition other than gender roles that keeps men from preparing the Sabbath meal.) It was my father who started the prayers and songs around the dinner table, led the services, gave the sermons in the synagogue, prayed three times a day at home.

But if Pop gave me song, Mom gave me poetry. She did not, however, read poetry. She spoke it. As prayer, a ritualized public form that can embody private feelings, gave comfort to my father, poetry was healing to my mother. She knew many poems by heart (an interesting expression, no? Isn't memorization an intellectual feat? Shouldn't we know poems by *head*?), and she used them in conversation. If I came home from school and greeted her with, "Hi, Mom, how are you?" she might well reply

> *Tired of these*
> *for restful death I cry*
> *save that to die*
> *would be to leave my love alone*

If I said, "Well, would you like to do something together this evening," her answer might be

> *Let us go then, you and I*
> *When the evening is spread out against the sky*
> *Like a patient etherized upon a table . . .*

I was not naïve. Like all teenage males, I knew I was sophisticated far beyond my years. I understood that all these great lines were written down somewhere, that it wasn't really my mom who had made them up and memorized them. (In case you're curious, it was Shakespeare, in Sonnet 66, paraphrased slightly, and T. S. Eliot; Ernest Dowson is on deck.) But it was definitely Mom whose answer to "Did you have a good night's sleep?" might be

> *Last night, ah, yesternight*
> *Betwixt her lips and mine*
> *There fell thy shadow, Cynara*
> *Thy breath was shed*
> *Upon my soul between the kisses and the wine*
> *And I was desolate and sick*
> *Of an old passion*
> *Yea, I was desolate and bowed my head*
> *I have been faithful to thee, Cynara*
> *In my fashion*

I miss my mom, who died in 1968, when she was fifty-five and I was twenty-four, after a long, painful battle with cancer. I find I no longer remember all the poems we used to declaim to each other, standing in front of the stairs, the piano, the kitchen door. My mind,

my mouth, my heart play tricks on me. If I commence with one of
the poems we shared, I can be short-circuited by a common rhyme
scheme, hurtling from one beginning to another ending, starting as
Edna St. Vincent Millay and ending as Matthew Arnold:

> *Love is not all; it is not meat nor drink*
> *Nor slumber nor a roof against the rain;*
> *And we are here as on a darkling plain*
> *Swept by confused alarms of struggle and flight,*
> *Where ignorant armies clash by night.*

Soliloquies, too. We were probably one of the few families
around, if not the only one, that would announce a swimming
trip by shouting, "Once more unto the beach!"

I know, I know, it's from Shakespeare's *Henry V*, it's his speech
rallying the troops just before the battle of Agincourt, and the
lines are really

> *Once more unto the breach, dear friends*
> *Or close the wall up with our English dead!*

But do you care, or do I? Or did my mom?

~~~

Here is what this personal history has to do with the role of culture
in creative community organizing. By the time I headed South in
1965, I was already in love with poetry and song. In addition to
what I'd learned from my folks, I knew some of the classic songs
that are part of the social justice hymnal through recordings by
Leadbelly, the Almanac Singers, the Weavers, Woody Guthrie,
Josh White. Seated in the cheap seats in the balcony, I even heard
Pete Seeger in concert. I saw the news reports on TV, watching as
the marchers on the highway from Selma to Montgomery, who
were beaten by horseback-mounted Alabama state patrolmen
wielding long lead-weighted clubs, linked arms and in the face

of appalling violence sang to keep up their courage, to overcome their fear.

Until I went South with SNCC in 1965, I wasn't aware that there was such a thing as political culture, or the extent to which it should be a regular item in any creative setlist. I didn't know that singing together can help people prepare to act and take risks as one, how much it can move and change our hearts, and reinforce our willingness to act in the face of fear and danger.

That is what, during the Southern Civil Rights Movement, these songs did, not just for southerners, permanent or temporary, but for all kinds of people who never set foot or voice in the South. They reached us in a deep, personal way, even though they are in a sense a language we do not completely understand, a language that can only be translated by the heart.

Like all prayers, the great political songs connect us across time. Who can stand swaying in a circle with arms linked, singing *We Shall Overcome*, and not be taken back to the Movement and to the South, whether they were there in person or in spirit, whether they were even yet born? But we hear with different hearts, according to when the song first came to us. African Americans, women, Latinas/Latinos, trade unionists, immigrants, lesbians, Native Americans, peace activists, gays, students each hear the song with the words and through the ears of their own movements.

We can trace the genealogy of *We Shall Overcome* in the labor movement from 1945, when striking African American tobacco workers in Charleston, South Carolina, recycled the old Christian hymn *I Shall Not Be Moved*, to when demonstrators protesting ICE raids today march, singing, "Unidos en la lucha/ no nos moverán." What matters when we close our eyes and link arms are the images that float before us: of picket lines, marches, demonstrations, vigils, jails. We hear the places we have been, ourselves and others like us, in the lilt and lift of the songs.

We hear the people we want to be. We hear, too, those who are *not* like us, the segregationists, gun thugs, police chiefs and sheriffs who so often blocked the way. They, too, are immortalized in the songs, frozen in time, caught as if by a camera in a fast-moving moment of history. If it were not for Florence Reece's unforgettable question in song, *Which Side Are You On?* who would ever remember Bloody Harlan's Sheriff Blair? Yet as our singing voices build, we swear again that we will *not* thug for J. H. Blair, in Kentucky or anywhere else, because we *are* for the union, we *know* which side *we* are on.

We hear also the people we have been. There is Ralph Chaplin, organizer and songwriter for the Industrial Workers of the World (IWW), the "Wobblies," just back from the West Virginia mine wars at the beginning of the twentieth century. What was it Mother Jones said that affected him so deeply? "You don't need the vote to raise hell"? "The Lord God Almighty made the women and the Rockefeller gang of thieves made the ladies"? "Pray for the dead and fight like hell for the living"? What was it about the South and southern workers that tears out of this Ohio-born organizer the amazing final lines to his enduring labor anthem *Solidarity Forever*, that are as fresh today as when he wrote them almost a hundred years ago:

> In our hands is placed a power
> Greater than their hoarded gold
> Greater than the might of armies
> Magnified a thousand-fold
> We can bring to birth a new world
> From the ashes of the old
> For the union makes us strong

He's right, you know. The union *does* make us strong. The truth will make us free. We *shall* live in peace.

And we *shall* overcome.

Strengthen the Story

In 1949, my father came to Liverpool
Seeking full employment on the Mersey docks
The war just four years over
And no work for him in Ireland
All he asked from England was a steady job
It's true that there were jobs, but it was only daily labor
Some mornings he was hired for the working crew
Sometimes a week went by
With hands deep in empty pockets
Adversity and poverty were all he knew

So my father and his comrades
Set out to march to London
To ask the King for justice for the working class
To tell him those who'd fought the war
Had died for more than England
And with the peace should come a steady job at last
The day they started marching
I stood beside my father
I thought he was the bravest man I'd ever seen
He knelt down unexpectedly
And set me on his shoulder
And we marched off together to confront the King

I do not know how far it is from Liverpool to London
I don't pretend that I recall each day and night
But when I close my eyes I can feel his face against me
As I rode into London on my father's pride
These days when oh so many
Look for work on every corner
When justice seems so distant and the way so fraught
I recall us marching and from high up on his shoulder
I see the better world for which my father fought

> We are carried on the shoulders
> Of those who came before us
> Such an over-used cliché
> Such a tired, empty phrase
> But my own father carried me
> From Liverpool to London
> On whose shoulders are we carried
> In these troubling days
> On whose shoulders are we carried
> In these days

*S*ometimes when I talk about how, as creative community organizers, we need to make sure that culture is a central part of everything we do, what I get back is, "That's easy for you to say. You're a professional musician. What about those of us who were told in high school choir just to move our lips and never sing a note? What if we can't even draw water out of a well?"

They often quote Emma Goldman: "If I can't dance, I don't want to be part of your revolution." (She didn't say this, but everyone believes she did.) "But," they continue, "she must have been a good dancer, or she'd never have said it. What if you're a community organizer with two left feet (or, I guess, for fairness, two right feet)? Where does that leave you except sitting in the cultural-political wallflower seats at the back of the high school gym?"

They've got a point. But they've also got a problem. If people are going to organize themselves, take risks, confront power, they need to feel at least potentially powerful. One of the best ways organizers can support the people we work with, as they struggle to build up their self-confidence, is by helping them *strengthen their stories*.

The stories we tell ourselves and each other about where we came from, the work our families did, their values, what they believed, stood and fought for—these also shape our own sense of who we are, of what we can and should do. Woven together, strand across different strand, they become part of the fabric that holds campaigns and community organizations in place.

One of the most effective ways to create this community fabric is through the strategic use of culture in its many modes: music, art, poetry, theater, the multiple methods human beings use to tell stories. Knowing how to do this is an essential skill for organizers.

You're right. That's easy for me to say.

So here's a suggestion. If you really are profoundly convinced that you have absolutely no musical or artistic talent, try applying a creative community organizing approach to the problem. Think about it as an organizational rather than a personal issue, and work to develop a collective rather than an individual strategy to resolve it.

That's what we've done at Grassroots Leadership, where I've worked for the last thirty years. So let me use this organization as a practical case study in how to make culture central to creative community organizing.

To start with, here is an old-fashioned visual:

We used this logo at Grassroots Leadership for many years—seven images set inside a traditional southern quilt pattern. Start with images of the economic reality that poor and working people confront: a factory with three smokestacks, pouring out smoke, perhaps about to close forever; a farm in distanced perspective, receding from view, much as family farms are disappearing all over the world. Go to the picture that depicts organizing for power, dark-skinned and light-skinned people together on a picket line. Observe the symbols of hope, of the future: a darker hand and a lighter hand either clasped or clapping; a stylized black and white palmetto, the state tree of South Carolina—or is it a rising sun?

Next notice the symbols of song and story. Folksinger/activist Pete Seeger's five-string banjo stretches its long neck diagonally across the square. Gospel and freedom singer Jane Sapp, at that time a Grassroots Leadership board member, sings or shouts in the upper-right corner.

Go back to the hands. If clapping rather than clasped, are they keeping time with the rhythm of what Jane Sapp is singing? Is Jane one of the people on the picket line, leading the song or the chant, shouting out the demands? Are the hands those of the people on the picket line, keeping time to the song, the chant, the sound of their feet as they march?

These seven images, along with the quilt itself, embody the intersection of creative community organizing and cultural work that is Grassroots Leadership's mission. They are also a fitting symbol of the way I've tried to work for the past forty-five years.

On the one hand, as a creative community organizer, my goal has been to help people who are marginalized, disenfranchised, and dispossessed build power for themselves and those like them, so that we can collectively achieve justice and equity for all.

On the other hand, I believe that power alone is not enough to win a just, equitable world. The experience of oppression does not necessarily make an individual, a community, or a nation wiser or more inherently democratic. When those who have been without power gain it, there is no guarantee they will exercise it more democratically than those who have had it before, or that their values related to race, gender, class, or sexual orientation, to take just these four examples, will be more enlightened, humane, or just.

Organizing alone, however creative, is rarely enough to change deeply held values and beliefs. To do that, we also need to use the cultural tools that throughout history have proved themselves able to break through to the human heart.

As organizers, we need to locate ourselves at that crossroads where activism and culture intersect, so that our work is rooted in both action and reflection. The dynamic tension between these varied ways of thinking and working will only give additional creativity and force to the work we do.

~~~

Organizing, in other words, must change more than power alone. It must also transform the relationship that the people being organized have to power. By integrating cultural work with traditional community organizing techniques, we can transform the nature of organizing and, through a process of celebration and community-building based in culture, art, and craft, help people change both their relationship to power, and how they think about and relate to themselves and to others.

People and their organizations may win on the issues. But that doesn't necessarily mean they develop new understandings of how and why they won, of power and how it's exercised, of difference and how it's exploited. They may experience the power of numbers, but not necessarily the concurrent power of knowledge, of understanding. Some of the conditions of their lives may change, but they will not necessarily transform their relationship to others (particularly their relationships to others different from themselves, to the "other"), to themselves, to power.

These transformations lie within the realm and are the responsibility of political education. Yet traditional organizing by itself isn't enough to create a transformative process that challenges anti-Semitism, racism, sexism, homophobia, and all the other barriers that divide people. Breaking through such rigid, resistant barriers requires velocity, momentum, torque, acceleration of the spirit as well as of the mind. It is a visceral and emotional as well as an intellectual process. Poems, songs, paintings, murals, chants, sermons, quilts, stories, rhythms, fabrics, pottery, dances can literally lift us out of ourselves, sometimes even into the life and consciousness of someone quite different from us.

The power of culture can also be an antidote to people's prejudices, their inability to see beyond their own eyes. If creative community organizing can transform power, culture can transform consciousness, can perform the acts of political education that when combined with action make social change transformative rather than merely instrumental.

Yet within the world of traditional community organizing, culture is too often a matter of "add music and stir" (to paraphrase Charlotte Bunch's famous quotation about women and history). Cultural workers and cultural work itself are often minor adjuncts to the organizing process: a quilt at an auction, a song at a rally, a chant on a picket line. Creative community organizing needs to draw on and incorporate the full power that culture can provide, the rich variety of traditional and nontraditional forms available to us: oral poetry, storytelling, *midrash*, meditation, quilting, guerrilla theater, preaching, drumming, unaccompanied song, silence.

Finding professional artists, making them allies, and learning to work with them in ways that bring not only their performing abilities but also their full artistic and political sensibilities into play should be a goal for all organizers and organizations. But it's also critical (and this is something at which many cultural workers and political artists are highly skilled) to call forth and highlight the cultural skills of ordinary people, the members and leaders of our organizations.

A remarkable number of people who in no way consider themselves artists nonetheless paint, draw, sing, write, act, quilt, create pageants, preach, dance. Creating opportunities for them to do so as part of an ongoing campaign or organization allows them to voice their rage and hope, to move from being silenced to being outspoken, to strengthen the stories they tell themselves and others. If the worker who says no to the boss from the opposite side of the negotiating table finds power and pride in that act, so does the community person who reads her poetry at the mass meeting before the negotiations begin.

How do we as creative community organizers move towards effective integration of cultural work with everything else we do? One answer is to add a set of basic tools to our toolboxes. It may or may not be true that everyone is in some way an artist. But every organizer can learn a handful of basic cultural techniques to incorporate into their everyday work. The many options include helping community members and leaders write songs, poetry, and chants (one hint: do it collectively in small groups, rather than individually), and using storytelling and theater to create strategy.

Here's one example of how to do this. It starts with a story, a piece of oral history told by Aunt Molly Jackson, radical midwife and union organizer from eastern Kentucky. I've memorized it, but it's just as easy to read the script (available at www.sikahn.com). The story takes place in a Kentucky coal camp in the 1930s, where the miners have been locked out, and their children are starving. Aunt Molly borrows an empty sugar sack from a neighbor, robs the company store at gunpoint, distributes the food to the families who need it the most, and goes home:

> *My house was the next house*
> *and by the time I got inside the door*
> *the deputy sheriff was there to arrest me*
>
> *And he said to me, he says,*
> *Well, Aunt Molly, what in the world, he says*
> *have you turned out, he says, to be a robber?*
>
> *I said, Oh, no, Frank, I said*
> *I am no robber*
> *But, I said, it was the last chance*
> *I have heard these little hungry children cry*
> *for something to eat*
> *'til I'm desperate*
> *I'm almost out of my mind*
> *And, I said, I will get out*
> *as I said*
> *and collect that money*
> *just as quick as I can*
> *and pay them*

I said, You know
I'm as honest
as the days is long

And the tears come in his eyes
And he said
Well, Aunt Molly, he says
They sent me up here, he says
to arrest you
The coal operator
well, Goodman, sent me here
to arrest you for that

But, he says
if you've got the heart
to do that much, he says
for other people's children
that's not got one drop
of your blood in their bodies, he says
then I will pay that bill myself, he says
and, he says, if they fire me
for not arresting you, he says
I will be damned glad of it
That's just the way he said it

He walked out
and he didn't arrest me

Aunt Molly's story makes for a great follow-up discussion, in part because it creates an organizing "case study," in which everyone shares the same experience and gets the same amount of information. I started using it when I was looking for a way to make training sessions seem more realistic, more like the actual situations organizers encounter in our work.

Discussions of potential strategies and tactics, I decided, could best be held in reference to an actual or constructed situation, when all persons participating had approximately the same degree of knowledge about what was going on. This information could be presented to the group by handing out a written document, showing a short film—or, it now occurred to me, using a narrative taken from oral history to approximate a real-life situation.

I begin this exercise by telling Aunt Molly Jackson's "Hunger" story in her own words. I then work with the group to analyze the situation: strategy, tactics, leadership, communication, empowerment, risk. We talk through the complex strategic and ethical questions richly presented by the piece. Is Aunt Molly Jackson an organizer or a community leader? Does she make good strategic choices? Is she acting ethically when she points a gun at the store operator? Does she put people in the community at risk without their knowledge or approval? Is that something organizers sometimes just have to do—or is it never acceptable?

At a certain point, the participants begin demanding to know what actually happened, so they can compare their ideas to real life. Given that Aunt Molly's story is about an incident that really did take place, that I'm a historian, and that from my days with the United Mine Workers of America I know many people who live and have lived, work and have worked in the coalfields, I could probably find out exactly what happened. But I decided it was better for the group—and for me—if I didn't know the answer. Instead, I say, "Well, let's find out," and turn the discussion into improvisational theater.

Since I only know the story as Aunt Molly told it, I ask the participants to treat the story as a half-finished script and to act out the roles as a way of figuring out what might have happened. Members of the workshop became Daisy and Ann, the mothers of the starving children; Frank the good-hearted deputy sheriff; Frank's boss, the "high sheriff"; Goodman the coal operator;

Henry Jackson, Aunt Molly's young son; Mr. Martin, the clerk at the company store; and Aunt Molly herself.

I act as the theater director to keep the action moving. I'll say, for example, "All right, Frank, why don't you go back to the jail now and explain to the sheriff why you decided to let Aunt Molly go free." When (in our extension of the tale) the high sheriff cusses Frank out and strides off to the coal camp to arrest Aunt Molly himself, I'll say, "Wow, it looks like Aunt Molly's going to be in jail for a while. Maybe some of you folks whose children are still alive on account of what she did ought to have a meeting and decide what you're going to do about that. Are you going to let her rot in jail after all she did for you?"

I never know how the scenario is going to play out. Sometimes Aunt Molly gets dragged off to jail after all, despite Frank's attempt at intervention and rescue. Sometimes the women get themselves together, storm the jail waving broomsticks and banging on frying pans, and free her. Sometimes the sheriff fires on the crowd and someone gets killed.

Whatever happens, we talk about it, analyze, strategize. In a short time, we share an experience almost like organizing, made all the more real because it incorporates oral history, storytelling, and theater. The cultural content makes the theoretical discussion come alive, pulls it down out of thin air and nails it to the floor.

Sometimes the participants say, "But none of us know anything about coal mining or coal camps." I try to get them to relate the situation to their own experience. "Okay," I say, "let's assume that instead of the high sheriff in the story we're talking about the local police chief, and that Aunt Molly Jackson robbed the all-night convenience store on the corner next to the projects." Once the story is reset locally, in terms of power dynamics that are already familiar, people usually overcome their resistance and jump back into the action.

Sometimes, I just plain get lucky. Once in Spokane, Washington, when someone said they didn't understand what it meant to be in a coal camp, I asked if anyone in the group had ever lived in a company town. I got three hands: an African American woman who'd grown up in a coal camp in West Virginia; a Mexican American woman who'd been raised in a copper mining town in Arizona; and a European American man from a hard rock mining camp in northern Idaho. We were able to talk, not just about mines and company towns, but about class differences and commonalities across lines of gender and race.

I believe that integrating creative community organizing and cultural work is something any organization can do to some extent—and that the progressive movement would be both more effective and more fun if this happened. But at the same time, we need to recognize that this challenge makes demands on the organization that decides to take it on. Just as culture flourishes best in an open society (although extraordinary and heroic art has been created under the most repressive conditions), cultural work is most at home in a democratic organization.

So organizations must strive to provide a set of expectations and attitudes that are conducive to creativity, whether in organizing or in cultural work. We should be proud of our work, but we should always be learning to do it better. We need to be as open and analytical about our failures as we are celebratory about our successes.

Don't be afraid to experiment. Within the world of community organizing, we need to extend our willingness to risk and fail. So don't feel bad if you don't have all the answers. I sure don't, and I try hard not to pretend that I do.

Many people believe that what successful organizers have is good answers. That's wrong. What we have is great questions. We're not in a community to *tell* people what to do, but to *ask* them. One of the greatest skills an organizer can have is the ability to frame and ask questions in ways that make people not only want to answer them, but also to think deeply, and in unexpected ways, about what the answers might be.

This is how some of the best strategic research takes place, and how some of the most effective strategies and tactics are developed. Communities of all kinds have a sophisticated understanding of the problems they confront, and often solid, practical ideas about what can be done to solve these problems.

But no one person knows even a major part of the answer. Imagine a giant picture puzzle, with each person having some of the pieces. Not only are they not sure where those pieces go, they don't even know how to start putting them together—and there's no photograph on the box the puzzle came in to guide them.

That's where the creative community organizer comes in: to help people work together to assemble the pieces, so that what they come up with makes at least reasonable sense to everyone who's been part of the process—and so that they feel a sense of ownership over what they have created together. At its best, this is not just a political, but a cultural process.

As organizers, we need to be eternally vigilant about recognizing and confronting issues of race, class, gender, sexual orientation and power, and many other issues that can be used to dehumanize and divide people. We need to learn, however, not just how to talk about these principles, but how to incorporate them into the work that we do every day.

How then do we work with people, how do we reach and teach them, in ways that transform their understanding of power and their relationship to it, not just individually, but collectively? How do we help them strengthen the story they tell themselves and others, so that they have the self-confidence and pride to stand up and struggle for what they want and need?

Combining organizing with culture and cultural work is part of the answer. It is at this intersection that the future of creative community organizing, and of all work for social justice, lies. We are, as the great Mississippi Delta blues singer Robert Johnson sang so many years ago, "Standing at the crossroads, trying to flag a ride."

Start at the Finish Line

I was hiding in the brush by the Ohio River
Sarah by my side, the baby in my arms
When the slave catchers found us
With our backs against the water
Winter come late, and the ice not formed
    And they sold me back South
    To the old Vann Plantation
    Two hundred miles from my home and kin
    To be buried in a grave with no marker on it
    Right on the spot where the new prison stands

I was walking the streets by the Anacostia River
But no one was hiring a young Black man
When the District police picked me up for no reason
Gave me 15 years for less than ten grams
    And they sent me down South
    To the old Vann Plantation
    Two hundred miles from my home and kin
    To be buried in a cell in a for-profit prison
    To make some men rich from the trouble I'm in

There were four million slaves from the African nation
Now there's two million prisoners
In the 'land of the free'
It might be right on this spot
That my great-great-grandmother
Had done to her what they're doing to me
        I can feel her spirit on the old Vann Plantation
        Beneath the towers and the razor wire
        All for the profit of some prison corporation
        If you say that's not slavery
        You're a goddamn liar

*L*ike so many other people, when somebody first told me that there were for-profit private prisons in the United States and elsewhere, I didn't believe them. As not only an organizer, but also a historian with a particular interest in African American, southern, and labor history, I knew that in the period following the Civil War southern states had hired out their prisoners to corporations that were industrializing the South, as well as to plantations that were reestablishing themselves. Prisoners mined coal, harvested timber, tapped trees on turpentine plantations, chopped and picked cotton, built roads, laid track, dug railroad tunnels, cut sugar cane, sweated in cotton mills. Called the "convict lease system," it was so brutal that each year an estimated one-third of these prisoners died, literally worked to death.

By the end of the nineteenth century, under pressure from progressive activists in the South and nationally, the last southern state had abolished its convict leasing system. Was it possible, I wondered, that at the very end of the twentieth century, on the verge of the new millennium, imprisonment for profit was back?

It was, with a vengeance.

It's not that everything was all right with this country's criminal justice and prison systems before the opening of the United States' first modern for-profit private prison in Houston in 1984. As the country approached the end of the twentieth century, prisons, jails, and detention centers constituted, to poor and working people of many races and ethnicities, a structural barrier comparable to that of legal segregation fifty years ago.

Think of the teenager—Latina/Latino, Appalachian white, African American, Native American, South Asian, Pacific Islander —who makes one mistake, a mistake that neither threatens nor hurts anyone else, and ends up doing five to ten years' hard time in an adult facility.

When that person, now no longer young, finally gets out from behind bars, they're not just an ex-prisoner. They are poor, deeply and desperately poor, and more likely than not will remain so as long as they live. Though some remarkable individuals overcome their years behind bars, the great majority are *de facto* barred for life: from employment, opportunity, stability, advancement. Any time in prison is almost always a life sentence.

Hard though it may be to believe, the "land of the free" currently imprisons more people than any other country in the world. With only 5 percent of the world's population, the United States has 25 percent of the world's prisoners. Of equal significance, we incarcerate at a rate that is on average five to six times that of any comparable nation. Right now, that adds up to over 2.2 million human beings.

But the issue affects more than just those in prison. Their mothers, fathers, sisters, brothers, partners, children, neighbors, friends, and other loved ones are all affected. Their neighborhoods and communities suffer the impact as well, both when they leave for prison and when they come back from it. When people have no hope and no prospects, the disempowerment they experience extends to the places they come from and return to.

The creation and growth of the for-profit private prison industry have helped create the radical expansion of incarceration that's taken place in the United States over the last twenty-five years. Current projections are that one in every fifteen Americans—one in every fifteen Americans!—will spend some time in a prison, jail, or detention center during their lifetime. That's twenty million people, more than the population of most of the world's countries.

The more prisons, the more prisoners. The more prisoners, the more long-term poverty and deprivation. It's as simple as that. A history of incarceration, whether in a prison, jail, or detention center, virtually guarantees lifelong poverty after release—assuming the person is lucky enough to be released at all.

Every time organizers help a community stop a prison from being built; close an existing prison, jail, juvenile or immigrant detention center; persuade a state to cut the funds in their corrections budget and/or to allocate public monies to alternatives to incarceration, we are helping to remove structural barriers to economic self-improvement for individuals and communities. Every person who, because of the work of creative community organizers, goes to a job or school instead of a prison, jail, or immigrant detention center represents a victory over poverty and inequity.

To suggest that, in the twenty-first century, poor and working people anywhere in the United States can change the conditions of their lives and communities without stopping prison expansion, reducing current levels of incarceration, and substantially changing the structural barriers erected by current U.S. prison and criminal justice systems and policies would be almost like arguing in 1950 that African Americans could achieve full political and economic equality without first dismantling this country's system of legal segregation.

~~~

The voice on the other end of the phone belonged to Gail Tyree, one of the most creative organizers I've ever worked with. Gail grew up in Florida and got a job with the phone company while still a teenager. Active in her union, the Communications Workers of America (CWA), she had worked her way up to president of her local. Eventually, she made her way to Grassroots Leadership, where she was now our Mississippi-Tennessee organizer.

"Si, you're not going to believe this one." Gail was breathing hard.

"I don't know if I will or I won't, Gail," I came back. "Try me."

"Are you sitting down?"

"I'm not, but I'll do it." I sat down. "Okay, go ahead. I'm listening."

"Corrections Corporation of America just offered Shelby County $30 million free and clear if they'll let them build a private jail here."

"They did *what*?" I was back on my feet.

Gail repeated what she'd just said.

"They can't do that. That's a bribe."

I could almost hear Gail shrugging over the phone. "Well, of course it's a bribe. But it's a legal bribe. They're offering the money to the county above board, not to some elected official under the table."

"What do they want for their $30 million?" I asked.

"Oh, nothing much." Gail could have been talking about what she had for supper. "Just a little old fifty-year contract."

I won't repeat what I said at that point.

When I finally calmed down, what I said was, "So what are we going to do?"

Gail didn't hesitate. "Fight them," she said. "It's what we do, isn't it?"

~~~

In every campaign, there is a magic moment just before the victory (and, unfortunately, sometimes just before the defeat). No matter how experienced and skillful we are as organizers, we usually never find out exactly when, where, or why that moment took place.

But we do know that it happened. It's the moment in which one person changes her mind.

In that instant, one corporate CEO says, "I know that many of you on the board disagree with me, but we're settling this right now. Furthermore, we're going to do it on their terms because, if we don't, it's only going to get worse."

In that moment, the vote on the county council stops being seven to six against us, and becomes seven to six for us—because one council member switched her vote.

In that flash, one lone person says, "Enough."

How do we as creative community organizers get from here to there? Ironically, we start by thinking about how to get from *there* to *here*. That is, we start the process of strategy development by imagining the instant just before victory, and then, working backwards, do our best to figure out the steps that will lead to that moment.

We usually don't know in advance who that one person is going to be. But, as we practice our craft, we can learn to become reasonably good at making educated guesses—and then at developing strategies for helping that person, whether or not we know for sure who they're going to be, come around to our point of view.

That's one of the fascinating secrets at the heart of creative community organizing. In order to move forward, we need to start at the finish line.

~~~

Gail Tyree met me at the Memphis airport.

"Where do we start?" I asked.

"Isaac Hayes," Gail said.

I couldn't have been more impressed. "He's working with us?" I asked. "That's amazing. How did you pull that off? How did you get to meet him? What did you say to him?" My excitement was uncontainable, and I had lapsed back into the rapid-fire verbal delivery of my northern childhood.

Gail shook her head. "Si, what makes you think I know people like Isaac Hayes? I wouldn't know how to find him if we were both lost." She grinned. "But I do know how to find his restaurant. He's got a rib joint downtown you really don't want to miss."

Gail was right. As I licked the last drop of barbecue sauce from my thumb, I agreed, "These are fine ribs."

"Si, we don't want you going back to North Carolina saying we didn't treat you right." Jacob Flowers spoke with a soft, almost sweet drawl.

I couldn't quite place the accent. "Jacob, where are you from?" I asked.

"I'm a Memphian."

"I don't care what your personal religious beliefs are." Gail had on her most serious look. "You're all right by me."

Jacob ignored us both. "Les, how do you like those ribs?"

"He's not going to answer you." Gail punched Les gently on the shoulder. "Les doesn't ever say anything unless he needs to."

Les nodded in agreement, gnawing on a rib all the time.

Jacob looked at the tall pile of almost bleached bones on Les's plate. "That's how he managed to eat twice as many ribs as the rest of us."

"He's smart that way." Gail had joined Jacob in staring at Les's bone collection, then shifted her gaze to her own much smaller pile. "We kept talking. He kept eating."

Les nodded again, still holding on to the rib.

Jacob moved his gaze up from the rib pile. "So where do you fit in all this, Les."

Gail didn't wait for Les to answer. "He's a Roman Catholic priest."

Jacob was trying hard not to look skeptical.

"He's a priest, not a saint," Gail explained. "If he wants to wear Hawaiian shirts and Bermuda shorts, that's his business."

Les stuck out his hand to Jacob. "Les Schmidt. Glenmary Order of Priests and Brothers."

"Les and I have been friends for forty years," I added. "His order loans him to Grassroots Leadership half time to help us work with the faith community. That's what he's doing here in Memphis."

Les nodded. "Glad to be here, too," he said, in a way that made it clear the introductions were over, and it was time to get down to work.

I caught Gail's eye. "So how does it look, Gail?"

Gail pushed her plate away. "Well, it doesn't look good, when you come right down to it. From everything I can tell, they've got the votes on the council pretty well sewed up."

"The city council?" I was trying to understand the local scene.

"No, the county council. We're still trying to figure out which way the mayors are going to go."

"Mayors?" I asked. Gail had clearly used the plural. "Memphis has two mayors?"

Gail shook her head impatiently. "Si, don't you know anything? There's a city mayor and a county mayor. Where have you been?"

I'd never heard of such a thing. "Kind of like the city mouse and the country mouse?"

Gail grinned. "Not country, county. See, we don't have a merged city-county government like you all do over in Charlotte. So there's a Memphis mayor and a Memphis city council. Then there's the Shelby County mayor and the Shelby County council. Do you think you can remember that?"

"I'll do my best, Gail."

"I'd appreciate that, Si. It would mean a lot to me."

"So who's got the power?" I asked. The question was meant for anyone. I looked around the table.

Jacob spoke first. "It's a county issue, Si. There are two facilities we're talking about. There's the Shelby County Jail, and then there's the Shelby County Correctional Center, which most folks call the penal farm.

"The Shelby County council has authority over both. They delegate the authority to run them to the sheriff. In the long run, though, the council makes the decisions. It's up to them to decide whether or not to turn it all over to Corrections Corporation of America."

"So where does the sheriff stand?" I asked.

"Between the two facilities, you're looking at about fifteen hundred public employees. Basically, when you come right down to it, they all work for the sheriff. That's a serious political power base, and right now it pretty much belongs to him. If they privatize, he loses it all. He's going to be careful, because he doesn't want to get on the wrong side of the real power people. But he's not going to support anything that undercuts his base.

"That's the case pretty much anywhere you look," Jacob continued. "Where sheriffs and police chiefs control the jail workforce, they're going to oppose privatization. But it's not about ideology— it has to do with preserving their personal and political power."

I turned to Gail. "You sure told me right, Gail. He's really good."

"Si, he's a whole lot older than he looks," Gail answered, looking warmly at Jacob. "He could be as much as twenty-four years old."

"Twenty-five," Jacob said.

"See, just like I said." Gail was on a roll. "But he's been running the Mid-South Peace and Justice Center ever since I got to Memphis, anyway. He kind of grew up in the business, if you know what I mean."

I looked at Jacob. "Gail means my folks are activists," he grinned. "It kind of runs in the family."

~~~

Well, and a good thing, too. But also something of a new thing, at least in the Deep South. There have always been a handful of courageous white antiracist southerners, voices of conscience in a tough part of the world. But they were the exceptions, rebels with an apparently hopeless cause, prophets crying out in the racial wilderness. But by 2006 it was no longer all that strange to find young white southerners whose hearts were in the right place, creative community organizers believing in and working to build something that seemed impossible in 1965.

I thought back to the last time I had been in Memphis. Forty-one years had passed since I drove my beloved '53 Chevy from Forrest City to the Memphis airport to pick up SNCC leaders Julian Bond and James Foreman and bring them back to Arkansas for a strategy retreat. Back then, white southerners tended to be more like the angry young men at the Wagon Wheel restaurant in Forrest City, staring furiously at half a dozen Black teenagers trying to eat their ice cream in peace.

Forty-five years ago, if Gail, Jacob, Les, and I, a Black woman and three white men, had sat down to eat in a restaurant in downtown Memphis, we would have been arrested.

Sure, many things were just like they'd always been. Racism was still raw. Poverty still clouded lives and dragged them down. But something basic had changed for the better.

Jacob Flowers was one of the young southerners helping make that change happen.

～～～

I was back home in Charlotte, talking to Gail on the phone.

"What's the count on the faith petitions?" I asked.

"We've got over a thousand signatures." Even over the phone, I could almost hear Les proudly laying the stack of petitions on the table. "We've got leaders from religions I didn't even know we had here in Shelby County." There was a serious sense of accomplishment in Gail's voice. "Les, how are we doing with the Wiccans?"

I could barely hear the rustle of Les's voice over the phone, but I couldn't make out what he was saying. I did hear Gail say, in mock horror, "No, no, they don't do that kind of thing here in Shelby County, Les. I think they're just some kind of weird Presbyterians."

"Si—Jacob, Gail, and I think that's enough signatures to go public." Les was trying to get us back on track. "We're planning a vigil in one of the largest churches in downtown Memphis."

"Black church?" I asked.

"No, that's what they expect." This was turning into a long speech for Les. "We want to show them how much white support we've got."

"How are the visits going?" I was running through my checklist of the various tactics we had agreed to use in the campaign.

Gail took back the mike. "Les and I have seen almost all of the ministers."

"How are you structuring the visits?"

"Like this. First, we show them the resolutions against private prisons that we've received from the Presbyterians and the southern Catholic bishops."

"We frame it as a moral issue," Les added. He and Gail were tossing the conversation back and forth between them, a technique I figured they'd probably worked out for when they went to talk with the ministers. "We don't try to argue the politics or the economics.

"Then, once they've warmed up to us, we ask if we could meet with them and the county council member who's a member of their church, just to explore the ethics of the situation together."

I was pleased, but slightly puzzled. "I thought you were having a hard time figuring out which churches some of them went to."

I could hear Gail chuckling. "Well, Si," she said, "some of these union correctional officers have their Sunday mornings off. It's in their contract, you know. So I asked them if instead of going to their regular church they'd like to go to church with one of the county council members."

"You did *what*?" I was having a hard time following.

"Well, since we didn't know which churches those particular county council members went to, we couldn't very well ask the correctional officers to meet them there, now could we?"

Okay, finally something made sense. "No, I guess you really couldn't."

"Right." Gail was having a good time telling the story. "So Les and I asked the correctional officers to follow them to church instead."

"Follow them to church?"

"Well, at a respectful distance, of course."

I was lost. "Gail, you're going to have to break this down for me. I don't get it."

"I told the correctional officers to park a little ways down the street from where the county council members lived and, when they saw them pull out of the driveway, to follow them to church."

Gail Tyree is a very creative community organizer.

Now I was the one laughing. I took a deep breath, trying hard to shift gears.

"So how does it look to the three of you?"

"Hard to tell. But two of the white Republican women are at least listening. They go to the same church." Les had climbed back into the ring. Gail must have tagged him. "Gail and I built a really good relationship with the minister before we asked him to arrange a meeting with them. He's helping us a lot."

"So, basically, you've got to get one of them to switch her vote."

There was a long pause.

"No, Si." It was Gail. "Les and I have been to see the six Black Democrats. No matter what we do, we're going to lose one of those votes."

"Which means?

This time, Gail didn't pause. "We don't need to get just one of those two Republican women to vote for us. We've got to get them both."

Be For, Not Just Against

I was interviewed last week on public radio
A man called up with something that I didn't know
My name is Grant, he said,
Here's what you need to hear
I'm a custodian—at least I was until last year

But now the jobs we did have all been privatized
Our lives, the public good, sold for the lowest price
A corporation does the cleaning work we did
They want the money not to help some troubled kid

Now we are standing at the edge of a forest of lies
Where all we hold in common has been privatized
Where corporations own every corner of our land
When everything is private, where will freedom stand

When those who only live for profit
Work to tear this country down
All we have to stand on is our common ground
And only we can find our way back home from here
We are custodians of all that we hold dear

*O*ne criticism community organizers run into goes like this: "Okay, we know what you're against. But what are you for? Are you just trying to tear things down, or are you working to build them up?"

Well, sometimes organizers *are* trying to tear things down, without necessarily trying to figure out what comes next. That's not always our responsibility. The courageous women who started the Women's Movement were concerned with tearing down the legal and social barriers that made women second-class citizens, kept them out of jobs, programs, and systems that were reserved for men, left them vulnerable to sexual exploitation and harassment.

The lesbian, gay, bisexual, and transgender warriors who fought the police at Stonewall were trying to stop violence against their community and its most vulnerable members. The brave women and men who, at great risk, built the Freedom Movement wanted to tear down a system of legal segregation that not only kept African Americans down economically and socially, but placed them at continuing risk of violence.

It was hardly supporters of the fight to end legal segregation who criticized the Freedom Movement for not always having answers to "What happens next?" Virtually all of the Movement's critics were fighting to *keep* segregation. Far from being constructive criticism, their attacks were a deliberate tactic designed to undermine and discredit a movement they hated and wanted to destroy.

Still, from a practical perspective, it's useful, as a part of any creative community organizing campaign, to be advocating for a positive as well as opposing a negative.

Gail, Les, Jacob, and I agreed that a good way to attack and discredit the proposed for-profit private jail, while being "for" as well as "against," would be to issue a research report. The document would suggest public policy changes that could save Shelby

County money. It would also recommend alternatives to incarceration for those unfortunate enough to be caught up in the criminal justice system that would be cheaper than putting them in jail. We would use the report to organize a "free media" campaign to raise awareness of the issue, both locally and nationally.

A multinational corporation would simply give an already sympathetic think tank a substantial sum of money to conduct "independent" research on the situation, as Corrections Corporation of America and the other for-profit private prison corporations had been doing for years.

Between Grassroots Leadership and the Mid-South Peace and Justice Center, we'd be lucky to scrape together enough cash to buy printing paper.

Gail wasn't worried. "We'll cross that bridge when we come to it. The question is, who are we going to get to write the report?"

I was back in Memphis now, eating breakfast with the team.

I thought a minute. "BBS," I said.

"I don't know, Si." Les was skeptical. "I don't think we can get the British Broadcasting Corporation interested in a local fight like this. Anyway, it's BBC, not BBS."

BBS, I explained, was another item in the creative community organizer's toolbox. It stands for "beg, borrow, and steal." It's how organizations with limited income survive. In the Brookside Strike, when I was organizing a "second front" in the Carolinas, I had called around the country and gotten over a dozen organizers to come help out for at least a month each. Now we needed to borrow some skilled researchers and policy analysts.

"I'm calling Bob." Gail already had her cell phone out. "We can probably steal him for a week, if I ask him nicely enough."

That's the "beg" part.

"Sure, no problem, Gail. I can drive up there first thing next week." Bob Libal is Grassroots Leadership's utility outfielder, as well as our Texas campaign coordinator, someone who can play just about any organizing position and do a good job at it. "But I don't know enough about jails to write that section of the report. You know, the part where we're going to recommend policy changes and alternatives to incarceration. We need someone who's a national specialist on jail policy. Like Dana Kaplan, if we could get her. She's the best. She knows more about jails than just about anybody."

Dana, now executive director of the Juvenile Justice Project of Louisiana, was at the time a Soros Justice Fellow with the Center for Constitutional Rights in New York.

We decided that a principled political analysis and argument was the only responsible way to approach her.

"Hey, Dana," Gail said over the phone. "How would you like a free trip to Memphis and all the barbecue you can eat?"

~~~

Multinational corporations often need to get some elected body to vote for legislation that will help them extend their reach and increase their profits. That body could be a city council, a county commission, a state legislature, or the Congress of the United States.

Right now, Corrections Corporation of America (CCA) needed the Shelby County council. They were working as hard as they could to get it and had made sure some of the main power brokers in the county would be on their side.

The white Republicans on the council were the easiest. Like so many Republicans anywhere in the country, their basic philosophy of government could be summed up as, "The private sector can do it better." Privatization is a natural for them.

Unions, on the other hand, were not in CCA's scheme of things. Moreover, AFSCME Local 1733, founded in the wake of Dr. Martin Luther King Jr.'s assassination by the same striking sanitation workers for whom Dr. King had gone to Memphis in the first place, wasn't just a union. It was a Black union, and a reasonably powerful one.

None of the seven white Republicans on the Shelby County council owed their jobs to African American votes. From every perspective, they were natural allies for CCA.

Not so the six Black Democrats. Some of them had a history of commitment to community and had been outspoken on labor, civil rights, and neighborhood issues. All of them were dependent on Black votes—and AFSCME had a history of delivering votes to its allies. The union's goodwill meant not just votes from the fifteen hundred employees at the two facilities, but from their children, parents, neighbors, friends, aunts, uncles—you name it.

Despite the white Republican majority on the Shelby County council, Corrections Corporation of America wasn't taking any chances, and was working hard to swing elements of the African American community behind their plan to build the new private mega-jail. Never mind that a great majority of the people who would spend time in it were young Black men, or that the radical growth in incarceration across the United States, by now spurred largely by the for-profit private prison industry, was stripping Black communities across the country of their young people, women and men alike.

So CCA rolled out their biggest guns. Thurgood Marshall Jr., son of the great African American freedom fighter and Supreme Court justice, had accepted a seat on the CCA board of directors, and he was spending time in Memphis lobbying the Black community to support privatization. So was Benjamin Hooks, past president of the NAACP, president of the National Civil Rights Museum, the elder statesperson among African American leaders in Memphis, whose family business had been promised a lucrative contract, should CCA win.

There were a number of constituencies in a position to influence the members of the county council, and they all had to be part of our plan. Gail and her team developed slightly varying arguments for the different constituencies they wanted to mobilize against the proposed jail, based on what they saw as each group's perceived self-interest.

For the AFSCME members whose jobs depended on keeping the facilities public, no argument was necessary. Their role was to bring the rest of the Shelby County labor movement into the fight, to help other unionized workers see that if CCA won, all public employees, and all union members, were at risk.

For the faith community, the moral argument was key. Over the past several years, primarily through work with the Roman Catholic Church and the Presbyterian Church U.S.A., Grassroots Leadership had honed that argument down to a fine edge, and we had a strong set of official denominational resolutions to back it up.

Convincing the Black business community which side they were on didn't take much talking. The public employees at the two facilities were not only their friends, neighbors, and relatives, they were among their best customers, earning salaries that were considerably higher than what most other African Americans in the county made. If, as usually happened when a jail or prison was privatized, every employee was terminated, and only some rehired, at significantly reduced wages and slashed benefits, that loss would be passed directly on to the Black business owners.

The white business community was more of a challenge. Businesspeople of a feather do tend to flock together, so CCA was a natural ally for them. But they also had a self-interest in promoting Memphis as a tourist destination. They had spent a long time trying to live down the legacy of Dr. King's assassination in 1968, not to mention the city's reputation as poverty stricken and racially divided. Now the city hosted the National Civil Rights Museum. You could stand and stare at the actual spot where Dr. King bled to death on the balcony of the Lorraine Motel, then tour the museum, moved and inspired by the raw courage and commitment of the young and old activists who had finally taken on and destroyed the system of American apartheid called segregation.

And oh, yes, they had a trinity for which any city anywhere in the world would have traded their best-loved mayor: B. B. King, Isaac Hayes, and Elvis Presley. Graceland was the number one tourist destination for hundreds of thousands of fanatical Elvis fans around the world, who came back year after year to worship at the shrine. Many nights of the week on Beale Street, historic home of the blues, the incomparable B. B. King held forth in his own club. When the music stopped, you could see how much damage you could do to a plate of ribs at Isaac Hayes's restaurant, as Gail, Les, Jacob, and I had so enjoyably done.

Memphis was trying hard. You could visit the old Sun Records studio, grab a microphone, and pretend you were there when Sam Phillips took a crew of what even the city's mostly racially righteous upper-class Caucasians would privately have called "white trash"—poor country boys with names like Elvis Presley, Carl Perkins, Jerry Lee Lewis, and Johnny Cash—and helped create rock and roll.

The old trolley cars had been brought back, each a different set of colors, nostalgia on wheels. There was the great river itself, the monumental Mississippi, so wide as it slid by the city that you could barely see across. But you could stand there on the shore and imagine Huck Finn steering his raft through the vicious currents, while his African American companion Jim, to whom Mark Twain never even gave a last name, hid under a pile of whatever was handy to evade the slave catchers hot on his trail.

Memphis, the white business leaders hoped and probably prayed, was finally coming back. What they definitely did not want, and absolutely didn't need, was another period like the one they'd gone through after Dr. King's murder.

So, to persuade them to use their influence with the county council, we would do our utmost to link, in the public mind, what was happening in 2005 to what had happened in 1968.

People around the world responded to our email blast asking them to write to the Memphis-Shelby County Chamber of

Commerce. We told them that if they had been thinking about possibly relocating their business to the area, or having their national association hold its annual conference there, or even just bringing the kids for a week's vacation—but now were concerned about what was happening and weren't so sure they wanted to go to Memphis after all—they should let the Chamber know.

We don't know how many letters, calls, or emails the Chamber of Commerce received. That's one of the challenges of creative community organizing. We come up with the best tactics we can, and we launch them out into the world, like carrier pigeons from a rooftop.

Then we wait. Sometimes we hear something, other times we don't. We just have to trust that, out there in the world, some of our tactics will eventually find their way home.

~~~

Then there were the elected officials. If they weren't going to oppose CCA, they at least had to be persuaded to stay out of the fight.

That's another core principle of creative community organizing. If you can't get a person or institution to support you, you want to do everything in your power to convince them that it's in their best self-interest to be neutral.

Luckily, most elected officials usually pay attention to which way the wind of public opinion is blowing.

Remember the old saying, "In the United States, any child can grow up to be president"? You're not going to find a lot of poor and working people who believe that. They're not even sure their children will grow up to be employed.

But there is one community left that absolutely trusts in the truth of that saying, and even takes that faith one step further, to the belief that, some day, they personally could become president of the United States.

Secretly or openly, all U.S. Senators, congresspersons, state governors, and big-city mayors believes this is their destiny. At a minimum, each is hoping and working to move at least one rung up the ladder: from mayor to governor, from member of Congress to United States Senator.

Whether it was true or not, everyone in Memphis and Shelby County assumed that both the city mayor and the county mayor had political ambitions. So, like the sheriff, both mayors were going to be very careful. Signing a contract with Corrections Corporation of America to privatize the county jail and the penal farm would have meant many things, but one of them could have been the near-destruction of AFSCME Local 1733. Although the mayors, like many elected officials in Shelby County and Memphis, had no love for the union, and would have been happy to have a freer hand in dealing with the county's public employees, neither of them wanted, in the middle of their own campaign for higher office, to be attacked as someone who tried to break Dr. King's union.

Finally, the remaining constituency we needed to organize were the young people, the students.

"Gail, this is so inspiring." I was practically beaming. "There must be a hundred young people here for the county council meeting."

"Thank you, Si," Gail answered. "We did our best."

"That was just brilliant, too, to have a couple of uniformed correctional officers present our report, where we called for fewer jail cells and more alternatives to incarceration." I couldn't have been more pleased. "Dana and Bob did a great job researching and writing our paper, but having the C.O.s present really brought it home."

Gail's grin was infectious. "Well, you know, we like to keep them guessing. Les, Jacob, and I figured they were probably expecting a couple of white hippies to present the report." She hesitated for a second. "No offense, Si."

"It's okay, Gail. I didn't take it that way. I know what you meant."

"Thank you." Gail was never anything but gracious. "You know, Si, those young people have come to every single meeting of the county council since we started the campaign."

Nothing could have made me happier—and happiness makes me talk too much. I didn't have a soapbox with me, but I sure was on one. "You know, Gail, so many folks my age are really down on young people today. They think they don't care, that they're only out for themselves, that all they think about is making money, they don't want to get involved. Yet, right here in Memphis, here's a hundred young people who are taking a stand for justice, who are . . ."

I stopped in midsentence. I had seen the embarrassed glance go from Gail to Les to Jacob and back.

"Okay, you guys, what did you do?"

"Oh, nothing much." The trio said it almost in unison.

"Come on, 'fess up." They looked around as if absent-mindedly, each waiting for the other to say something. Finally, Les broke the silence.

"Well, Si, you know we did a lot of work with the local colleges, and with the Memphis Theological Seminary, back when we were starting the campaign." Les could have been delivering a sermon at Sunday Mass.

"Huh."

Now it was Jacob's turn to play attorney for the defense. "A lot of the professors really like what we're doing. They think it's an important lesson in how democracy works, or doesn't work."

"Uh-huh."

Jacob couldn't suppress his grin. "So we got the professors to give their students credit for sitting in the county council meetings."

I covered my eyes with my hand. "They get course credit for just sitting in the meetings?"

"Not for just sitting in the meetings." Gail's air was almost professorial. "For helping pack the hall every time the council meets."

"Si, they do have to write a paper about the experience." Les, face serious, was summing up the argument for the jury. "They don't get credit just for sitting there."

Gail Tyree, Les Schmidt, and Jacob Flowers are three very creative community organizers.

~~~

This time, the barbecue joint was in Austin, Texas. Jacob and I were sitting at the table across from each other.

"That looks like really good barbecue." He was staring wistfully at my plate.

"Jacob, I'm so sorry," I said. "But I understand those scientists who do genetic engineering are working really hard on a vegan pig. One of these days, all this will be yours."

"At least the local beer is good."

It was. We clinked bottles.

"Well," I said, "if anybody ever earned a couple of beers, we sure did. It was a great victory."

Jacob looked thoughtful. "The amazing thing is that it's still going on. They're actually taking our recommendations for policy reform seriously, at least some of them. They even gave the Mid-South Peace and Justice Center a seat on the committee that's looking at all this. We've got a seat at the table."

"So we didn't just stop something bad, we helped start something good."

"That's exactly right." Jacob put his beer down on the battle-scarred table. "Si, can I ask you something?"

"That depends on what it is."

He ignored me. "When you first got to Memphis, did you think we had a chance?"

I laughed. "No. Absolutely not."

"No chance at all?"

"Maybe one out of fifty. No more than that."

We both paused for a swallow. Jacob went on, "So why did you argue so hard for taking it on the way we did?"

"It's like what Gail always says. It's what we do." I put my beer bottle down on the table. "You know, when we take on a campaign, there's never any guarantee that we'll win, or even break even. But, if we don't take it on, we get an absolute guarantee."

Jacob looked straight at me. "And that guarantee is?"

I met his eyes. "If we don't take on the fight, there's an absolute guarantee that we lose every time."

He nodded. "Anything more than that?"

I thought for a minute.

"Well, it's also who we are, isn't it?"

We sat quietly for a minute or so. It was getting late. I had an early flight back to North Carolina in the morning. It was almost time to call it a night. But I had one more question.

"Do you think they'll be back?" I asked.

Jacob laughed. "Si, you know better than to ask me that. Of course they'll be back. You think they're going to give up just because we beat them once? They've got too much at stake in Memphis—and they don't like losing."

I grinned. It had been a rhetorical question, and I'd been caught asking it. But I hung in there.

"So, when they come back, what are we going to do?"

Someone from the wait staff was passing by. Jacob caught their eye and held up two fingers, then turned and looked me. His smile was beatific.

"Same thing we did the last time, Si." The sheer joy in his face lit up our dark corner of the barbecue joint. "It's who we are. It's what we do."

Find the Glue

We were the world's first colony
We yet may be its last
Five hundred years ruled by another land
The violence, the cruelty
The stealing of our past
Who dared to hope that peace might be at hand?

Five centuries have hardened us
To struggle and resist
'Til neighbors seem like enemies, not friends
Until one day we find within
The courage to desist
From violence that grows and never ends

If those who prayed for violence
And shed their children's blood
Can work for peace that lasts beyond all time
Then enemies in other lands
May some day staunch the flood
Of war that breaks all hearts, both yours and mine

    The Irish sea that sheltered us
    And sometimes kept us safe
    Still breaks its heart upon the English shore

> But when the storm is over
> And the sea lies wide as dreams
> Then peace will rise
> From these green hills once more

*M*y first serious encounters with the role of race in organizing came during the summer of 1965, working with SNCC in Forrest City, Arkansas. In Centre County, Pennsylvania, where I had lived until the age of fifteen, I almost never saw anyone who was a person of color, with the exception of the athletes who were just beginning to arrive at Penn State to play football and basketball. Certainly, anyone in any position of power or authority was white.

Now, everything was reversed. The leaders of SNCC and of the Southern Civil Rights Movement nationally were almost all African Americans. The local leaders of the Movement in Forrest City were all Black. The local SNCC project leader was Black, as were the great majority of the SNCC staff and volunteers. The community we lived in, that sheltered, nurtured, and protected the SNCC workers, was exclusively Black. Beyond the boundaries of the Black community lay white communities, which offered only threat and danger.

The visible national leaders of SNCC, some of whom occasionally arrived in Arkansas from headquarters in Atlanta, who spoke with us and framed the Movement in broader political terms, were Black: James Foreman, Julian Bond, John Lewis, Stokely Carmichael. So were the heads of the other major national civil rights organizations: Dr. Martin Luther King Jr. at SCLC, James Farmer at CORE, Roy Wilkins at the NAACP, Whitney Young at the Urban League.

I am speaking now of my view in the summer of 1965, at the age of twenty-one, of how that particular world looked to me as someone whose main Movement job was doing carpentry in Freedom Centers and repairing cars and mimeographs, the now-extinct copying machines that preceded the Xerox generation. Later, with the benefit of hindsight and history books, I came to understand some of what was less visible. Women leaders of SNCC and of the Movement, such as Ella Baker and Fannie Lou Hamer, were excluded from formal organizational positions, even as they exercised extraordinary leadership and influence. Some whites also played leadership roles, but generally not as visibly as those who were Black.

Among these white behind-the-scenes activists was my uncle Arnold Aronson, my mother's older brother, whose work over many years helped inspire and shape my own. Arnie was one of three cofounders of the Leadership Conference on Civil Rights (LCCR), the nation's oldest and largest civil rights coalition, together with the great labor leader A. Philip Randolph, president of the Brotherhood of Sleeping Car Porters, and NAACP national president Roy Wilkins.

Arnie worked behind the scenes with all the great African American leaders of the Movement—King, Lewis, Young, Farmer, Wilkins, Randolph—on many critical strategies, campaigns, and events. Yet he was never a public spokesperson for the Movement. In fact, for the rest of his long life, in which he continued to work on civil rights issues, he refused to speak or write about what he had done in the 1960s, believing that in a progressive democratic movement that appropriately belonged to African Americans, the role of the white participants was to support that movement, not to lead or speak for it.

My uncle's salary was paid by the National Jewish Community Relations Advisory Council in New York, where he lived, but he spent the week in Washington, D.C. Our family had recently moved from Pennsylvania to Chevy Chase, Maryland, just across the District of Columbia line. Orphaned together at relatively young ages, Arnie and Mom were understandably quite close, so he stayed with us whenever he was in town. At night, Arnie, Mom, and Pop would sprawl across the bed and chairs in my parents' bedroom, and he would tell us what had happened in the day's meetings and discussions.

Many of the high-level strategy meetings took place at the Shoreham Hotel, an elegant brick and wood structure in downtown D.C., with a long curving porch studded with rocking chairs. It wouldn't have looked out of place on a southern plantation. In fact, Washington in those days was very much a southern city, with "white only" and "colored only" drinking fountains within sight of the U.S. capitol.

When I was home from college, I served as Arnie's chauffeur. His eldest son and I share the same first name—in traditional Jewish families, children are never named after a living relative, lest the Angel of Death confuse the two and take the younger by mistake—but after those who have passed on. My cousin and I were both named after our grandfather, Arnie and Mom's father, Simon Hirsh Aronson. To avoid confusion, Arnie and his spouse, my aunt Annette, called me "Cuz" and their oldest by the name he and I shared.

"Okay, Cuz," he'd say when I picked up the ringing phone, "I'm ready. Come get me."

I'd drive down to the Shoreham and insert my '53 Chevy into the line of limousines waiting in the hotel's long curving driveway. One by one, the uniformed chauffeurs would step outside their elegant vehicles, stand facing the hotel's front doors, and announce, to take the then vice president of the United States as an example, "The Honorable Hubert Humphrey." On one occasion, I did the same, standing outside my battered vehicle in my own SNCC uniform of blue jeans and work shirt and proudly announcing, "My uncle, Arnold Aronson."

I never got to meet any of the famous leaders of the Movement, except for one lunch at Arnie and Annette's house with Roy Wilkins. Wilkins arrived driving a bright red sports car, an MG-TD as I recall. I was excited to meet him, but appalled that he owned what to me seemed such an expensive car. I had just come up from Arkansas, and I complained to my uncle that one of the national leaders of the Movement should be driving such a beautiful vehicle when my sisters and brothers in SNCC were risking their lives daily.

"Drop it, Cuz." Arnie spoke firmly. "He's earned it."

~~~

Given how extraordinarily hard it is to build multiracial organizations even today, when we supposedly live in a more racially enlightened period than we did almost fifty years ago, how do we explain the willingness of so many whites in the Southern Civil Rights Movement to accept the leadership of African Americans? Of course, not all whites accepted that leadership. Many resented it, rejected it, challenged it, tried to exercise their white power and privilege, attempted to take over leadership.

But, that reality aside, how do we explain the participation of whites in the Southern Civil Rights Movement at all, given the historic reluctance of so many white progressives to participate in movements led by people of color? What was I doing there anyway?

Personally, I find it difficult and a little dangerous to try to explain forty-five years later why I did whatever I did way back then. The temptation to revisionism and political correctness is always there. Memory is misleading at best, even in the short term. But, whatever I said or felt at the time, here's what I now think was really going on.

To start with, I was deeply influenced by peer pressure. Even on primarily white campuses, being involved in the Movement was a cool thing to do: picketing, marching, getting arrested (very cool), occupying buildings (really cool—I did it, I know), "going South" (the coolest of all).

I was also lucky enough to be raised by parents who were passionate about racial justice. For them it was an expression and an extension of their religious beliefs. Mom and Pop were outraged by the injustices done to African Americans in the United States, and they were outspoken about civil rights.

At the same time, Pop in particular was adamant that he and Mom were "not political" and were simply "doing what's right." (Unlike the parents of "Red Diaper Babies" I met for the first time in SNCC, so called because their parents were members of the Communist Party, my folks were at their most radical registered Democrats.) In going South and joining SNCC, I was doing what my parents had raised me to do, even if I terrified them by doing it.

Mom and Pop also both came from large extended families that lost heavily in the Holocaust. They understood in their gut the dangers of any authoritarian racism. While my folks never said this explicitly, the message I felt and learned clearly was, "If this can happen to Black people in the United States today, it can happen to Jews tomorrow."

No one ever said this to me directly. But I'm convinced that emotion was absolutely there, not just in our family, but throughout the North American Jewish community. The Southern Civil Rights Movement began only fifteen years after World War II ended, partly because of the energy and anger brought back to the United States by returning African American war veterans. For Jews whose memories of the Holocaust were still bleeding wounds, the response of white racists to the Southern Civil Rights Movement must have been terrifying: the mobs, the Klan, the American Nazi Party; the dogs, guns, sneering sheriffs; the violence against children as well as adults, the burnings, the murders.

Besides, the enemies of African Americans were usually also enemies of Jews. My mother remembered how during her childhood, at the cottage in New Hampshire they rented one summer, the Klan had come and set up a burning cross on their front lawn. Frightened by the rise of right-wing racism but also proud of the resistance put up by southern Black communities, how could so many Jews not have been moved?

To be clear: My parents were careful not to confuse the level of U.S. anti-Semitism in the 1960s (real, not to be taken lightly, but not an everyday problem for most Jews) with the level of racism against African Americans (out of control, virulent, violent, deadly, an immediate daily threat and danger to every Black person). But they understood the Civil Rights Movement, not just as "their fight," but as "our fight."

As a creative community organizer, I am always trying to figure out people's common self-interest, the glue that binds political organizations and movements. My own personal self-interest, as a white Jew in a movement led by African Americans, was in seeing that the systems of violent repression being used against Black people were stopped in their tracks, before they spread to me and my family. It is no accident that the overwhelming majority of the white participants in the Southern Civil Rights Movement were Jewish—estimates range from 50 percent up, at a time when Jews made up less than 3 percent of the total U.S. population.

But however much I and other Jews, as well as other whites, may have seen the Movement as "our fight, too," it really wasn't our fight in any immediate self-interested sense. Whites active in the Southern Civil Rights Movement were concerned with ending segregation, with strengthening democracy. Blacks were concerned with economic and physical survival, with staying alive. Only in occasional moments were whites in the Movement really threatened with physical violence: on integrated picket lines, in restaurants (but only when eating with Black coworkers or when recognized as civil rights workers), in confrontations with the law and with vigilantes. Beyond those moments, we could step back into our white skins, disappear into the anonymity and privilege of whiteness. In many cases, we were stepping back into class privilege as well. Only a few white civil rights activists came from families that shared the desperate poverty of most southern African Americans.

Thinking back forty-five years, I believe I also had a second self-interest: that of all those who dream of a better world, a more democratic society, a more just economy, who feel rightly that every injustice in some way diminishes them as well—a moral self-interest, if you will.

I inherited that dream from my mother. Mom believed passionately in the possibility of racial justice, that people of different races and ethnicities could and should work and live together, not just out of economic self-interest, but in real friendship and love. I believe she intentionally raised me to do something to help make her dream real in the world.

It's a great inheritance—and a hard one to live up to. Given the many reasons that so many people of color and whites consistently find *not* to be in social or personal relationship with each other, building solidarity across this wide divide requires a set of self-interests so overwhelming that they can overcome the inertia and antagonism built up over many years. Put crassly, at least in the South, many white people and African Americans would just as soon not have to deal with each other in serious ways, and will only do so if they absolutely have to.

So you have to find the glue that will help people stick together.

In my work as a creative community organizer, I've seen this happen in two ways.

The first is what I think of as "defensive organizing." In this situation, a community is confronted with a threat, often from the outside, something that could at least partly destroy that community's quality of life: a toxic or nuclear waste dump, turkey or hog farm, slaughterhouse, prison, high-voltage power line, polluting industrial facility. To the extent that members of the community see this as a threat, they will mobilize to keep it from happening. To the extent that the community includes different racial groups, they will at least in the short run work together.

But such unity is usually short-lived. Because such situations are defensive in nature, and because the timetable is largely controlled by outside forces, things happen very quickly. The community needs to mobilize with remarkable speed if there is to be an effective opposition. So there is rarely the time and space to do the critical work of storytelling, interpersonal exploration, celebration, and discussion that can build understanding and unity across racial lines, and create a shared political understanding and agreement that is potentially transformative. Because the issue that brings community members together is limited, so is its potential. Even if an organization is founded to deal with the situation, it is not likely to survive beyond the immediate issue and campaign.

If the organization does survive, it is unlikely to have a broad political perspective, since it was originally organized around a very specific goal. It was built to stop something rather than to start something. Winning means that the community's quality of life will not get any worse, not that it will get better.

The second situation in which I've seen whites willing to participate in political movements led by people of color is where there was a common and ongoing economic self-interest. That's the glue.

I learned some of my most important lessons about the importance of finding the glue while working as a union organizer in textile mills across the South in the late 1970s. A basic principle understood by both the mill companies and the union was that African American workers were much more likely to support organizing drives than white workers. (This was before the great influx of Spanish-speaking workers into the South and the textile industry, another constituency that could be counted on to be strongly pro-union.) Generally, in a union representation election supervised by the National Labor Relations Board (NLRB), you could count on 80 percent to 90 percent of Black workers voting for the union.

Both labor and management had figured this out. Management's response was to establish a de facto ceiling of about 40 percent for African Americans in the workforce—go higher and you were virtually inviting the union organizers to town. If we could get about 80 percent of the Black workers to vote for the union, we only needed about one-third of the white workers (20 percent of eligible voters) for victory.

What this also meant was that while African American workers were a minority in the plant, they were a majority within those actively working for the union. So the union organizing campaign required a coalition across racial lines. If racist and anti-union traditions among white workers were too strong, they didn't participate and the union lost. If their desire for dignity and respect on the job, fairer treatment, better wages and working conditions was strong enough to outweigh their reasons *not* to be in a union with Black workers, then the union won.

These objective conditions made it easier for me to take on racial issues directly. Black workers would say to me, publicly or privately, "Look, why do we need the whites? They're racists. They don't really want to have anything to do with us anyway. If we start with the Black workers, focus on the issues that we care about most, like racism and discrimination, we can really mobilize and get the union in."

I'd point out that, under U.S. labor law, you need 50 percent of the votes—and there weren't enough Black workers in the mill to get to that number. Further, I'd say, of course we want to deal with racism and discrimination. That's part of what the union stands for. But if we don't make the campaign broad enough to include issues that white as well as Black workers care about, the whites won't have any reason to want a union—which means Blacks won't be able to get one, either.

White workers would say to me, privately or publicly, "Look, why do we need the Blacks? Most of the workers in this mill are white anyway, enough to win a union election. But they won't join the union because they don't want to be part of something that Black people control. You need to start with the white workers, make it clear that's who the leaders of the union are going to be, and we can get those union cards signed like crazy. We've got nothing against the Blacks joining the union, but it's just not going to work if they're in charge."

I'd point out that, under U.S. labor law, you need 50 percent of the votes in an NLRB-run election for the union to be certified as the bargaining agent for rank-and-file employees in that particular workplace. Because of the anti-unionism endemic to southern white mill workers since the violent failures of union organizing from the 1930s through the 1950s, white votes alone were never going to be enough in a mill that was 40 percent Black.

Furthermore, I'd say, the union is for everyone. It's not just for Blacks and not just for whites, but for all workers. If the company discriminates against a Black worker because they're Black, the union is going to stand up for them, just as the union is going to stand up for any worker who's being pushed around by management. Take it or leave it. Either everyone gets a union or no one gets one.

~~~

There's an old civil rights song that starts, "They say that freedom is a constant struggle." This is true of all creative community organizing, and certainly of efforts that require bringing whites into organizations, campaigns, and movements led by people of color.

A delicate balancing act takes place within the organizing committee and organization. Generally, my experience is that having about two-thirds people of color and one-third white people in the room, on the committee, on the board, on the picket line works best. If there are proportionately too many white people, people of color perceive, usually correctly, that they will eventually be pushed out of leadership and power. If the number of white people drops significantly, whites will decide that this is a "Black thing" (or a Latino/Latina thing, or a South Asian thing, or a Native American thing), and not for them. It's worth noting the irony of these dynamics: Most whites seem to think having 10 percent people of color in the room is fair representation, but that having 10 percent white people in the room means people of color have taken over.

Having a significant majority of people of color helps ensure that leadership stays in those hands. But it also makes it easier for people of color who are not in the leadership to participate. When people of color are in the majority, not just power but culture shifts. By reversing the usual ratio of participation and power in the dominant society, we open up the doors and the windows.

Perhaps because race so much defines the history and politics of the South, most southern organizers carry this consciousness with them. Among other things, southern organizers count. Ask organizers from most parts of the country what the racial balance in a meeting was and they'll answer either "pretty good" or "pretty bad." Ask southern organizers and they'll give you an exact breakdown of how many people of color and how many whites were there, usually broken down by gender as well. When planning a meeting, an action, a leadership election, they'll consciously strategize so that a good racial balance (usually meaning a people of color majority) is maintained.

For example, at Grassroots Leadership, where I've worked since 1980, at least two-thirds of the board members are people of color. I believe that on any racial justice issue the white members of the board would be passionate advocates and would vote for the right thing. But if the board were to split on racial lines, people of color control two-thirds of the votes. For me personally as a white founding executive director, it meant that my power could be counterbalanced and, if necessary, overruled. If whites are to play leadership roles in democratic movements, this kind of counterbalancing is both healthy and critical.

The same dynamic applies to gender. The Grassroots Leadership board consistently has at least two-thirds women on it. Again, if I were on the wrong side of a gender issue, I believe that the men on the board would vote against me. But, should some or all of them choose not to, the women have a clear enough majority to force the decision.

For all of us who want to see truly multiracial progressive democratic movements, we need to look for issues that create this possibility. Again, that's the glue. For example, in 1996 Grassroots Leadership started organizing against the privatization of public assets in several southern states, including the growth of for-profit private prisons, in part because the transfer of public goods and services to private profit-making hands undercuts the well-being of both people of color and whites.

Over time, we focused our anti-privatization efforts on the criminal justice system. Within the broad movement against the prison-industrial complex, a movement led primarily by people of color, we carved out a specific organizational niche by creating organizing campaigns that focus on the abolition of for-profit private prisons, jails, and detention centers, including immigrant detention centers. Grassroots Leadership's statewide studies on "Education Versus Incarceration," which document the link between increasing public dollars for prisons and decreasing funds for higher education, are an organizing tool specifically designed to help build bridges across racial lines.

Of course, what goes around comes around. The same links and principles that make progressive democratic organizing possible can also be used to undermine and oppose progressive policies. In several local campaigns to stop for-profit private prisons from being established, we've sometimes been defeated by multiracial campaigns. Both Blacks and whites, desperate for jobs, have seen private (and public) prisons as their only alternative and have fought to bring them to their communities—despite being well aware that their main use would be to warehouse young men, and increasingly women, of color.

We need, then, to be sure from the beginning that not only our processes but also the policies and goals we work towards help create the possibility of multiracial unity. How, in the real world of creative community organizing, do we actually do this?

Because so few people have successful experiences in working multiracially, there is also a real lack of knowledge about what to do and how to do it. When it comes to multiracial organizations and campaigns, there's still work to do to develop the basic tools of the trade: the checklists, the do's and don'ts, the places to be watchful and careful, the insights and intuitions that can guide organizational work. We also lack the theories that hold these elements of practice together, that make sense of the small details of daily work, that give them unity and coherence.

If we're really going to make a difference, we as organizers need to develop and refine theories and practices, principles and techniques that we can use to resolve differences among people of color and white people. Learning to use these principles will help us build internally strong and viable community-based organizations, which can also work together to create vibrant, creative networks and coalitions. In addition to the focus on race, special attention has to be paid to issues of gender, class, sexual orientation, and distribution of power, which in turn also affect racial dynamics.

Such a theory and practice can only be developed over time, by the combined work of many people and organizations. But it is helpful to have a number of hypotheses to test against our developing knowledge, some ideas with which we can argue, some points of departure for our action and reflection.

In this spirit, let me offer as a starting point some preliminary principles for multiracial organizing. Organizations that want to address racial conflict and to build unity across racial lines need to take these principles into account and establish, or reestablish, them internally.

- An *institutional* as distinct from a personal commitment to racial equity that is clearly and forcefully stated

- An *analysis* of the organization's purposes that demonstrates convincingly that these purposes cannot be met without equity

- *Issues* that connect both the common and the differing self-interests of people of color and white people, that are of sufficient immediacy to overcome the substantial forces working against unity

- *Leaders*, both people of color and white people, who are personally committed to racial equity

- A *political will* shared by all participants to enforce the structures and rules relating to equity, even under enormous pressure

- *Structures* of both governance and administration that share and/or rotate leadership and decision-making power among people of color and white people, and which help ensure that white people must accept the leadership of people of color, not just vice versa

- *Equity* as a clear principle in agreements on division of all other resources, including money, power, seniority, job security, access, and publicity

- *Internal education*, aimed at both white people and people of color, that deals explicitly with both positive (equity) and negative (racism) issues

- A *common opposition* as well as common issues: often what unites us is not only what/whom we are for, but what/whom we are against

- *Processes* that, at all levels, demonstrate the institutional commitment to equity: how and where meetings are held, how and to whom information is circulated, how and when decisions are made

- *Safe spaces* within which these processes can be worked through, places to meet and talk where people of color and white people feel equally comfortable and powerful— along with the recognition that no space is fully safe

- *Culture* that is balanced among people of color and white people and that is comparably accessible to each: norms of public and private speech, food, music, humor, art, history, stories

- *Social occasions* as well as public events in which both personal and political relations can develop

- *Consistency* in and among principles and practices, along with the attention to detail that helps ensure their continuity

- *Mutuality* among people of color and white people in terms of responsibility for all of these principles, practices, and processes

Perhaps it's time to revisit the words of the old civil rights song, "Black and white together, we shall not be moved." Maybe it's time to be moved, to move ourselves and others, within our constituencies and across constituency/racial lines. Maybe the beloved community of which Dr. King spoke is not something we reach some day in the future, but something we experience a little bit every day while, as creative community organizers, we walk and work towards it.

Learn Your Limits

Down in the darkness, down at the breaker
Close on the midnight hour
Steadily working, quietly leaving
Trailing a thin line of powder
The little Schuykill Valley town is all lit up tonight
By flames that lick like tongues from the breaker fire
The tight-lipped Coal and Iron Police
Won't get much sleep tonight
Looking for the sons of Molly Maguire

Down in the tavern, banded together
Strong men are hiding their sorrow
Over at Pottstown, there at the prison
Ten men are hanging tomorrow
I only tried to organize the men I worked among
But I'm hanging in the morning, will you miss me
And Monday early, so they say, the mines will open back
The Coal and Iron Police are drinking whiskey

Down in the darkness, standing together
Ten men are lined on the gallows
Holding a red rose, waiting for sunrise
King of the Mollies, Jack Kehoe

The trap is sprung and Molly's sons
Are traveling into time
Murdered by the men who hope to hang her
But the unborn souls of union men
Are all with her tonight
And the Pennsylvania pits are dark with anger

*W*hen people find out I've spent forty-five years working as a civil rights, labor, and community organizer in the Deep South and Appalachia, often the first thing they ask is, "Did you experience a lot of violence?"

I suppose this makes sense as a way of introducing yourself. In the United States, one of the first things people ask when they meet someone new is, "What do you do for a living?" In many countries, such a question is considered the height of rudeness. But, hey, we're a young nation, and our public manners still have a ways to go.

Set in that context, "Did you experience a lot of violence?" is at least a reasonable opening gambit. But it's not a question I generally want to answer, particularly when I suspect that the person asking the question is in danger of romanticizing violence, and will be happiest if I look off into the distance, a troubled expression on my face and, after a long apparently painful pause, simply nod my head yes.

I usually escape by saying that as far as violence goes in my life as an organizer I've been remarkably lucky, and then change the subject. It's true that I've personally experienced very little violence—certainly almost nothing compared to truly courageous people like John Lewis, today a leader in the U.S. House of Representatives, and a major force for all things good. As chairman of SNCC during the Southern Civil Rights Movement, Lewis probably held the record for number of times arrested, beaten, or both. In the front line of marchers crossing the Edmund Pettus

Bridge in Selma, Alabama, during the Selma-to-Montgomery march in 1964, he was clubbed so badly by Alabama state troopers on horseback that he ended up in the hospital with a concussion.

But it's also true that I've been in some situations, especially in the 1960s and 1970s, where the threat of violence hung over every day's work. This was particularly true in the Deep South during the Southern Civil Rights Movement, and in the Appalachian coalfields. It didn't often happen to me—but it certainly did happen.

Far too often, the violence was not simply a threat, but a reality. Ask anyone close to the Southern Civil Rights Movement, and they can recite from memory the names of some of those who were murdered as part of southern segregationists' struggle to preserve what they saw as their way of life. We will call out their names like a litany.

Emmett Louis Till was brutally lynched in 1955 at the age of fourteen in the small Mississippi town of Money for allegedly whistling at a white woman.

Addie Mae Collins, Carole Robertson, Cynthia Wesley, and Denise McNair—young schoolgirls—were killed in the 1963 bombing of the 16th Street Baptist Church in Birmingham, Alabama.

Forty names are engraved on the black Canadian granite of the Civil Rights Memorial in Montgomery, Alabama. These are just the dead we know, not the hundreds who died anonymously. There is a little-known but wrenching fact related to the 1964 disappearance of James Chaney, Andrew Goodman, and Michael Schwerner, three civil rights workers, an African American and two Jews, who were kidnapped, shot at point-blank range, and buried beneath an earthen dam in Philadelphia, Mississippi, in June 1964. During the massive search for the three young men, the would-be rescuers dragging one of Mississippi's many dark rivers pulled up the body of an African American who had obviously been murdered. The newspapers described him as "unknown."

To history, perhaps, but not to the Black family who waited in vain for him to return home, an all-too-common condition in the Deep South in those violent days.

Life in the coalfields was also tense, the potential for violence endemic, and the outcome sometimes startlingly brutal: Witness the murder of Lawrence Jones on the Brookside picket line. If not everyone went armed every day, they kept a rifle, shotgun, pistol, or revolver near at hand in their home, women and men alike.

Here's how seriously the UMWA took the potential for violence. I'm not a particularly big person, but I'm not what you'd call small, either. In those days I hit the scales at about 170 pounds, and stood about five feet ten, closer to six feet in the cowboy boots I had started wearing in a futile attempt at protective coloration.

Though the UMWA organizers at Brookside didn't exactly weigh in each morning, like I used to do when I wrestled in high school and college, my guess is I was the lightest of the lot by some sixty pounds, and the shortest by at least six inches. They were amazing human specimens, men who had worked underground since they were youngsters, with biceps and triceps as hard as the coal they dug, that swelled the arms of their T-shirts to an extent that made me green with envy. Temperamentally, they were some of the warmest and most thoughtful people I've ever met. Visually, they could stop a coal truck.

The UMWA sent bodyguards to Harlan County to protect them.

The lead bodyguard was a coal miner named Rich Hall. Rich wasn't any larger than the organizers, but he was a karate expert, and unbelievably fast. We'd be sitting in one of the trailers the union had rented in Jones' Trailer Park in Harlan, drinking beer, spitting tobacco, and, as that good southern expression goes, "talking trash."

One moment you'd be sitting on the raggedy sofa that passed for furniture in the UMWA organizers' trailer, with Rich relaxing in a chair opposite you, at least eight feet away. A second later he'd be sitting next to you. You never even saw him cross the room. He was that fast.

One day when we were going through our usual post-work male rituals, Rich turned to me and said, "Si, can you crush a beer can with one hand?"

I felt my biceps and triceps swell. Moments like this don't require speech, just a nod. I nodded, then nodded again for good luck, twice in quick succession.

"Show me," Rich said.

In those days, beer cans were still made from steel, not aluminum or some soybean derivative like they are today. One-handed beer can crushing was a reasonably serious test of manhood.

I drained the beer I had been drinking and placed the empty can in my right hand. Looking Rich straight in the eyes, I squeezed.

The beer can crumpled. I felt like I had just won a gold medal in the Olympics.

Rich shook his head scornfully. "Not like that," he said.

He emptied his beer can, set it on the table, and gripped the top rim of the can with his four fingers and thumb.

"Like *this*." Slowly, steadily, he drew his thumb and fingers towards each other.

The rim of the beer can shivered for a moment, then gave up the ghost and collapsed into a tiny point.

~~~

The closest I ever came to serious injury during my forty-five-year organizing career was not on a picket line or freedom march, but in Granny Hager's living room, on the banks of the Kentucky River in Hazard—you guessed it—Kentucky. (In the southern mountains, the term "Granny," like "Aunt" in Aunt Molly Jackson, is a mark of deep respect and admiration for a community elder—not, as when applied by whites in the Deep South to African Americans, a derisive, sneering insult.)

Granny was an old white woman, leaner than a split locust fence rail, and twice as tough. She was at least in her eighties by then, and the coal companies paid tribute to her long history of fighting them tooth and nail by giving her a hard time at every opportunity.

It was a process in which they showed themselves to be remarkably creative community harassers. Granny's house sat on a narrow strip of land between the river and the railroad track. Every night, the coal company would leave a train with a hundred gondolas hooked up to it—at least a mile long—in front of her house.

To get from the road to her house, Granny had two choices. She could either walk all the way to either the locomotive or the caboose end of the train, cross the tracks, and then walk back along the other side of the tracks until she got to her house—a long hard trip at any age, especially in the dark and carrying a sack of groceries. Or she could, as she always did, crouch down and, on her hands and knees, crawl under a coal car from one side of the track to the other, from the road to her house.

I don't know how many of you have had the experience of crawling under a coal car in the dead of night, in eastern Kentucky or anywhere else. I don't recommend it. Everyone knew the coal company was capable of anything, especially when it came to Granny Hager—including deciding to move the train suddenly. Had I been there at that moment, it would have been very hard for my friends to explain to my family what had happened to me.

In those days, our children were still too young to go to school, so they could travel pretty much anywhere with me. I had one of those old Dodge vans with the engine between the two front seats, covered by a flat metal cowling. I took the legs off two fiberglass kitchen chairs, bolted the seats to the engine cover, and hooked up a couple of seat belts, so that the kids could ride along, one in front of the other.

Our oldest son Simon was five at the time and in that particular young male developmental stage when firearms are a prime object of desire. When he noticed what he thought was a cap pistol lying on the small table next to where Granny Hager was sitting, his eyes lit up. He reached for it, picked it up, swung around, and, with that wonderful smile he still has, aimed it directly at me, his index finger on the trigger.

I couldn't see down the dark barrel, but I did see the bullets in the ancient .32 revolver's chambers pointing straight at me. I am no Rich Hall, but I have never come out of a chair and across a room so quickly in my life.

Stories about violence, and even potential violence, are seductive, aren't they?

~~~

Speaking of seduction: One early afternoon, back when I was working with SNCC in Forrest City, Arkansas, Mrs. Brown came by the Freedom Center.

"Got a minute?" she asked.

I nodded.

"Come over to the house with me."

Mrs. Brown's house was one of the few buildings in the Black community that had two floors. When we got inside, she stopped at the foot of the stairs leading to the second floor where she slept, and turned to look at me.

"Come upstairs," she said.

I hesitated. SNCC workers, female and male, were often approached by community members with something more than freedom on their minds. But, as far as SNCC's principles were concerned, local folks were strictly off limits. Any experienced organizer will tell you that getting mixed up romantically with a community member is not just a bad idea, but a serious violation of professional ethics, like a psychiatrist sleeping with a client.

"Come," she said again, and started up the stairs.

~~~

Before I finish this particular story, some background may be helpful. I had by now grown more or less used to the South's love affair with firearms—although I do know it isn't restricted to the South, that even female governors of Alaska are subject to the contagion.

Several years before I went South to join SNCC, when I was still in my late teens, I was hitchhiking across Texas. I was picked up by a middle-aged white man driving a beat up pickup truck. He looked me over carefully as he slowed almost to a halt, and finally decided to stop, right next to me. I opened the passenger side door and climbed into the cab.

"Thanks," I said.

"Don't mention it," he replied, ignoring the fact that I already had. "Just don't try anything."

The only thing I was trying was to get back to my parents' home in safely suburban Maryland. I had been out on the road for a couple of months, traveling by thumb through the United States and Mexico, sleeping in graveyards and county jails, and that was way long enough.

"No problem." I answered, hoping that would end the conversation.

It didn't. "You know why you'd better not try anything?"

Feeling a direct yes or no answer was probably too definitive under the circumstances, I made a discreet noise in my throat to indicate that I didn't.

"Open the glove compartment."

I stretched forward and flipped open the lid.

"See that pistol?"

I did. In fact, I was seriously shocked to see it. I'm not sure that I had ever seen any sort of firearm up close before. While I'm sure there are at least a few Jewish deer hunters out there somewhere in the American heartland, generally speaking, it's not our thing. It would be at least somewhat unusual, for example, if the person sitting next to you in the synagogue whispered, "Hey, what do you say when Rosh Hashanah services are over, we hit the woods, and see if we can't bag us a ten-pointer?" It's probably happened at some point in our history, but I'm personally not aware of it.

Even in my temporary state of shock, it did occur to me that if there was "trouble," whatever that meant, I was a lot closer to the glove compartment than he was. If he really was worried about me "trying something," pointing out that there was a pistol inches away from me didn't seem very smart on his part.

But keep in mind, all this was new to me. I was a rabbi's son from up North. What did I know from pistols?

I felt some sort of response was required. "How come you carry a pistol in your glove compartment?"

He'd been staring straight ahead at the road, hands tight on the steering wheel, ever since I'd stepped into the truck. It wasn't really necessary in that part of Texas, since there was no chance whatsoever that the road would bend even slightly in the next five hundred miles, but that's what he was doing. Now he turned his head to the right, looked directly at me, and said, "On account of there's so much violence around here."

This happened a good twenty years before I married feminist philosopher Elizabeth Minnich, who has helped me partially overcome my understandably irritating organizer's tendency to always go directly to strategies and tactics. These days, I occasionally venture into, if not thinking philosophically, then at least reflecting briefly before speaking. Still, I knew even then there was something deeply wrong with his logic.

Nonetheless, I decided it was just as well not to say anything. The old truck sped on into the Texas night.

In the South, you see a lot of bumper stickers commenting on firearms. One very popular one reads, "I'll give up my gun when they pry it from my cold dead fingers."

It has occurred to me that if you were the driver of a vehicle bearing that bumper sticker, and you knew that someone out there desperately wanted you to give up your gun, that is not particularly good advice to give them.

Another popular bumper sticker reads, "Guns don't kill people. People kill people." Okay. But what do most people who kill people use to kill them? I rest my case.

In Forrest City in the summer of 1965, rifles and shotguns were everywhere: resting against the wall in a kitchen or living room, leaning against a bed, hanging in a rack over the front door of a house or the back window of a pickup truck, slung over a shoulder as the shoulder's owner meandered down the road.

So I wasn't all that surprised, when I walked into Mrs. Brown's bedroom, to see a lever action .30-.30 rifle with a scope lying on the bed, right next to a box of cartridges. Strangely enough, I was relieved. If this was going to be a seduction, it was going to be a highly unusual one. I decided that wasn't what this was about.

"Look out the window." She spoke politely, but it was an order. I obeyed.

"What do you see?"

"Nothing much. Just the street and some houses."

"What time have you got?"

I looked at my watch. "2:51."

"Wait two minutes. He never misses."

Sure enough, exactly two minutes later, at 2:53 P.M., I saw a police cruiser rolling slowly down the street. Even behind the shades, there was no mistaking the face.

"Jim Wilson," I said. The police captain was the most vicious and violent man on the Forrest City force, with a reputation for using his power to rape African American women.

Mrs. Brown nodded. "He comes by here every day like clockwork, right at this time."

She walked over to the bed, picked up the rifle, and stretched it out to me. "Here. This is for you."

I didn't know what to say. "What am I supposed to do with it?"

Mrs. Brown looked straight at me.

"Kill him."

It is a measure of how traumatic that moment was that, to this day, I have no idea what happened next: what I said, if anything, what I did, other than that I got out of there as quickly as I could, leaving the rifle lying on the bed, feeling more than a little sick to my stomach. I have some vague recollection of Mrs. Brown arguing that this would mobilize the people who had been silent too long, but that makes no sense. The killing of a police officer by a civil rights worker, white or Black, would have led to unbelievable retribution and violence against the Black community. It had happened many times before, with no provocation. It would certainly happen again.

Telling this story, I am still trying to understand what happened and why. Had Mrs. Brown been one of the women Wilson had dragged into the back seat of his patrol car? Had this happened to a sister, a mother, a daughter, a friend? In the midst of a nonviolent movement, had something suddenly snapped? Or had she been waiting for years for someone who could be the agent of retribution, and had come to see me as that particular Angel of Death?

~~~

I said earlier that I usually avoid telling stories that involve violence or potential violence, because I don't want to romanticize it. I don't want those of you who are thinking about becoming organizers to think that the potential for violence in some situations makes the job exciting or heroic.

It doesn't. It makes it terrifying.

I decided to write these stories down now—not standing alone, but with commentary—because, too often, organizers are unjustly accused by those in power of inciting violence.

That's a lie, and it needs to be put to rest.

Still, the rumor is out there, and I don't want this job to appeal falsely to those who are attracted to danger at best, violence at worst. I want people to become organizers because they are peacemakers, passionately committed to finding ways human beings can solve the very real problems that confront and divide us, without doing damage to each other.

Put simply, there is no place in any kind of organizing for violence, or the threat of violence. If that's what you're looking for, don't come here.

But I want to be very, very clear that, in ruling out violence, I am by no means backing down on my lifelong commitment to nonviolent direct action, to confrontation, to conflict when absolutely necessary. I believe we must first do everything we can to achieve consensus, to find a solution that works and saves face for everyone. We need to do everything in our power to, as Dr. King in his "I've Been to the Mountaintop" speech so eloquently quoted the Old Testament prophet Amos, "Let justice roll down like waters, and righteousness like a mighty stream."

But when the intransigence, the deep-seated prejudice, the drive for obscene wealth, the self-interested arrogance of those in power make compromise impossible, we should, as Dr. King did, confront them with all the nonviolent fierceness we can muster.

To raze a slumlord's property to the ground; to drive an exploitative enterprise such as a for-profit private prison corporation or a predatory lender out of business; to make sure a sexual harasser is fired—that is not violence.

It's called justice.

Expect the Impossible

The man called T. Don Hutto
Must have been some kind of man
'Cause he's sure got a man-sized share of fame
It's not just anybody gets their name put on a building
Where children are held prisoner in their name
The town of Taylor, Texas is not an hour from Austin
But when you're there you're in a world away
Look inside the prison yard
Just beyond the chain link fence
You will see young children at their play

You might well stop and ask yourself,
What have these young children done
To be sentenced to such painful loss and fear?
It's all because their mom or dad
Was caught here without documents
Like twelve million others living here
Now you may think all immigrants
Should go back where they came from
And if they don't—hell, let 'em rot in jail
But if it was your own daughter in a cell at T. Don Hutto
With your grandchild in her arms, how would you feel?

What would you do if your own four-
Or six- or eight- or ten-year-old
Was growing up in prison like these kids
Since when in these United States
Do we put kids in prison
Because of what we say their parents did
Call it "family detention,"
Say "We do it for the children"
You're lying to yourself down to the roots
But call it playing politics
With children's lives and sanity
You're getting somewhat closer to the truth

So if you're down in Austin
Take the highway out to Taylor
Bring some good friends with you for the ride
You might even wear a flag pin
To show you still believe in
The dream for which so many fought and died
Step out onto the highway, turn to face the prison
Stare at those walls 'til you forget your name
Say a prayer for T. Don Hutto
Say a prayer for all those children
Then close your eyes and hang your head in shame

*I*f I'd been surprised in 1996 when I first learned there was such a thing as for-profit private prisons, I was completely astounded ten years later when I heard one of them was being used to imprison immigrant children as young as infants and as old as seventeen in cells together with their parents.

This was happening, not in some military dictatorship, not in some feudal monarchy, not in some warlord-run country, but right here in the United States of America. In the small rural town of Taylor, Texas, just thirty-five miles northeast of Austin, Corrections Corporation of America had opened its T. Don Hutto Residential Facility, the first private for-profit immigrant family detention center in the country.

Almost from the moment the first families were sent to Taylor in May 2006 and children were locked up with their parents, Grassroots Leadership's Austin-based organizers started working with a long list of local, state, and national organizations to shut Hutto down, and to get the kids and their parents out of detention. I had listened at meetings of our national staff as our Texas campaign coordinator Bob Libal and our Texas organizer Luissana Santibañez talked about the strategies and tactics they and our partners were developing for the campaign. But the situation itself was so unbelievable, so outrageous, so absurd that it took a while for the reality of what was taking place to hit me emotionally.

I remember the moment it happened. In April 2008, I traveled to Montezuma, a tiny town in the northern New Mexico mountains where Grassroots Leadership's southwest office is located. We were having a board-staff retreat, and our friend, filmmaker Matthew Gossage, had just finished introducing *Hutto: America's Family Prison*, the seventeen-minute film he and Lily Keber had recently finished.

Light dimmed in the room, then brightened on the small portable movie screen. As the camera traveled past the Texas State Capitol, under green and white overhead signs to Interstate 35, past miles and miles of barely rising and falling fields, some brown and barren, some bright with crops, the captions on the screen rolled by, in Spanish and English:

30 miles north of Austin, in the small town of Taylor, Texas, lies the T. Don Hutto facility. Once a medium-security prison, this "residential facility" now houses a new kind of prisoner: immigrant families.

Citizens from over 40 countries have been held in Hutto. They come to the U.S. fleeing persecution, violence and poverty.

With 512 beds, T. Don Hutto can hold 200–300 families a day, including pregnant women and nursing infants, in the largest trend of family internment since WWII.

The camera moves in on a family group. Denia is a former Hutto detainee from Honduras (the film omits the last names of formerly incarcerated speakers to protect them from retribution). Pregnant at the time of her detention, she holds her recently born son in her arms. Her youngest daughter Angie, four years old, sleeps against her shoulder. Her oldest daughter Nexcari, who is nine, sits next to her, wide awake. Denia speaks first:

> To tell you the truth, I was really scared. I would say, "Dear God, What am I going to do with a newborn in here?" He would die in this freezing cold. It was so cold, and the worst thing was, they wouldn't give us enough blankets. I thought we were going to die because of the situation. Or how could I get enough rest if I was prohibited to rest here? I wouldn't be able to take care of myself properly the way one should after giving birth. I couldn't have there. To tell you the truth, I was very worried.

The off-camera voice asks, in Spanish, "Do the children suffer much?" Nexcari answers, in the same language, translated into English in the subtitles:

Yes. They suffer a lot. And at the same time they cry because they think that the guards are going to take their moms away.

For me, it was terrible, because every night I would dream that they were scolding my mom, and were taking her to another jail. ...They told us that moms that misbehave, and hide cookies in their pockets, would be sent somewhere else, and that they were going to leave their children here, that they were going to separate the children from their moms.

Denia and her children were incarcerated at Hutto with about one hundred and fifty other families. Between May 1, 2006, and May 23, 2009, over thirty-eight hundred children, women, and men from more than fifteen hundred families were detained in the for-profit facility. Every single one of these parents had been imprisoned with their children in the cells at Hutto for a minor civil violation: being in the United States without the appropriate documents, a condition they shared with twelve million other people.

Why had this small group of children and parents been targeted for detention? What had happened, in the United States and in Texas, that we were now forcing young children to grow up in prison?

Well, for one thing, ICE, the Immigration and Customs Enforcement division of the Department of Homeland Security, was trying to make an example of them. This appalling strategy, which flies in the face of all ideas about equal justice, was based on the mistaken idea that imprisoning a small number of children together with their parents would deter other families from migrating to the United States. In effect, it punished one group of families in an effort to change the potential behavior of migrating and asylum-seeking families around the world.

In fact, increased family detention, militarization, and privatization along the border had the exact opposite effect. Large numbers of seasonal workers who came annually to the United States with legal work visas were no longer sure whether, if they went home, they would be able to return the next year. So they stayed, even after their visas expired. As a result, the number of undocumented immigrants went up rather than down.

For another thing, President George W. Bush and his advisers had decided that anti-immigrant rhetoric and action was an effective way to help elect and reelect their conservative friends. The raw anti-Black ranting that had sustained and reelected right-wing white politicians for so many years, most heavily in the South but also in other areas of the country, was no longer publicly acceptable. Given the millions of African Americans who had become enfranchised since the Voting Rights Act of 1965, many of whom were concentrated in key congressional districts around the country, it also constituted a form of political near-suicide.

But the old raw racist rhetoric wasn't really gone. It had just been replaced by heavily coded "tough on crime" language. Being seen as tough on crime would, at the very least, help you get elected or reelected; being labeled as "soft on crime" would almost certainly get you defeated.

So, even though immigration is in no sense a crime, candidates could ramp up their chances for election by adding immigrant bashing to their arsenal of law-and-order campaign rhetoric. Although these candidates rarely talked specifically about the race or ethnicity of the "illegal aliens" they were attacking, everyone knew exactly about whom they were talking.

Another reason for the sudden growth of immigrant detention, including immigrant family detention, was that it involved very big money for the for-profit private prison corporations and their shareholders. Here, for example, is Steve Logan, at the time CEO of Cornell Corrections, speaking to investors on a conference call shortly after 9/11:

It can only be good . . . with the focus on people that
are illegal and also from Middle Eastern descent. . . . In
the United States there are over 900,000 undocumented
individuals from Middle Eastern descent. . . . That's
half of our entire prison population. . . . The federal
business is the *best* business for us . . . and the events of
September 11 [are] increasing that level of business.

But it wasn't only the private prison corporations who saw
themselves as benefiting from the immigrant detention boom.
Small towns and rural areas throughout the United States, which
forty years ago would have fought tooth and nail against having
any kind of prison, jail, or detention center located nearby, were
now fighting even harder to get them. Made desperate by the loss
of jobs and the departure of their young people for greener urban
pastures, these towns and counties had come to see immigrant
detention centers as their only hope for economic stability. José
Orta, an activist in Taylor, Texas, where Hutto is located, had it
exactly right when he said,

A lot of people in Taylor saw it as an economic boom
for the community. Most small towns that were losing
manufacturing jobs were looking for a way to create
something stable. Prisons for profit are very profitable.
But they're not profitable to the community that they're
based in. They're profitable to the shareholders of that
corporation.

Even in Taylor, despite intense community pressure to go
along in order to get along, principled local activists like José Orta
raised their voices against having a private for-profit immigrant
family detention center located in their community. Across Texas,
the voices swelled to a chorus. Week after week, students, faith
leaders, trade unionists, immigrant rights organizers, teachers,
activists working on a dozen different causes traveled to Hutto
from across the state to demonstrate, to show their solidarity with

the families on the inside. Stretched out along the highway across from the chain link fence that separated the children and their parents from the world, they held up signs that read "A two-year-old is not a terrorist," "First they came for the Muslims," "Texas shame," "Prison is never in the best interest of a child"—all the time chanting, "Close Hutto now! Close Hutto now! Close Hutto now!"

You rabble-rousers, you activists, you quiet lovers of justice: Don't ever let anyone tell you that demonstrations were only effective in the 1960s, that in the twenty-first century we need to find other ways to make our voices heard that are less, well, confrontational. For the most part, those who say that now aren't the ones who were on those civil rights, feminist, LGBTQ, labor, and anti-Vietnam war picket lines. They were on the other side, building their careers rather than the Movement. If they were in fact part of the Movement at that time, but are now trying to gain prestige and wealth by denouncing what they and the rest of us did—well, we know what such people are called.

The initial phase of the campaign to close Hutto, between 2006 and 2008, was effective because it was a cooperative coalitional effort, bringing together organizations with a wide range of skills, experiences, and expertise. The first vigil at the detention center took place in December 2006, organized by Grassroots Leadership and Texans United for Families (TUFF), and preceded by a three-day walk from the Texas Capitol by Border Ambassador Jay Johnson-Castro. A lawsuit brought on behalf of ten of the families by the University of Texas Immigration Law Clinic and the ACLU, which represented Hutto detainees in immigration court, not only improved conditions, but also brought media attention to what was going on inside the facility.

The Women's Refugee Commission's report *Locking Up Family Values* focused a microscope on conditions at Hutto, further raising the campaign's profile. Courageous members of the Family Justice Alliance in Williamson County, where Hutto is located, helped organize dozens of vigils at the facility. The Free the Children Coalition organized caravans and brought people to the vigils month after month from San Antonio, South Texas, Houston, Dallas, College Station, and other areas of the state. Amnesty International helped organize a large Hutto vigil in June 2007 for International Refugee Day.

Watch the film *Hutto: America's Family Prison*, and you'll see the continuing power of mass demonstrations and cooperative direct action campaigns. Here is Luissana Santibañez, at the time a student at the University of Texas and a Grassroots Leadership organizing intern, now a member of our staff, pounding on a drum and shouting out for justice. Here is former Hutto detainee Elsa, testifying on the makeshift stage:

> I was in there for six months, and it was one of the saddest things to see my children suffer in there. Unfortunately, my children weren't the only ones there. There were many other children suffering, very many. Just imagine being locked up 24 hours a day, and seeing your children say, "Take me out of here."

Now Texas Indigenous Council leader Antonio Díaz is on the stage, his passionate voice stirring up the crowd:

> They cannot be seen behind those walls. So we're here to let ourselves be seen and counted. And saying "We care." We care. We care enough to want to shut it down. We cannot stand silently by and not denounce those prisons for profit that are right there in front of us. And they're all around our state right now. These people are not criminals. No criminal charges against them at all. They're refugees. Crimes are being committed against them.

He's right. We do care. We care a lot. That's what it means to be an organizer, a community leader, a member of the Movement.

But was all the care in the world enough to shut Hutto down, when set against the combined forces of ICE, the Department of Homeland Security, the Bush administration, Corrections Corporation of America, and the for-profit private prison industry?

<center>~~~</center>

Like many of my coworkers and friends, I hoped that help would come via the election of Barack Obama as president of the United States. Immigration reform was clearly going to land squarely on the new administration's table. Trying to analyze the dynamics of the situation, I almost persuaded myself that the new administration might, in its first hundred days, actually move to close Hutto and end immigrant family detention. There were political points to be scored by being seen as tough on undocumented immigrants, I figured, but very few to be gained by locking up four-year-olds.

Meanwhile, with help from Grassroots Leadership and our many allies, Hutto was well on its way to becoming a national and international scandal. An article by Margaret Talbot in the *New Yorker* on March 3, 2008, titled "The Lost Children," helped raise Hutto's profile and concern for the families imprisoned there. Needless to say, it didn't exactly help Corrections Corporation of America and their good friends at ICE when the *New York Times* reported that Jorge Bustamante, a special representative from the United Nations, was denied access to Hutto. Bustamante did manage to interview some of the detainees after their release, and said,

> There was public information, complaints about the violation of human rights to children. And children are part of the most vulnerable migrants in the whole context of human rights. I heard a three-year-old asking his mother, "Mom, why is God not helping us? If He is so powerful, why he doesn't tell these people that we are not bad people?"

Corrections Corporation of America and ICE may have barred Bustamante from inspecting Hutto, and they certainly refused to give an interview to filmmakers Matthew Gossage and

Lily Keber, as well as many other members of the media. But ICE apparently failed to pass the word to all of their staff members that they should at least try to show a little discretion and good judgment when dealing with the public. It's kind of fun to imagine their reaction when they heard the recording of the interview that ICE regional spokesperson Nina Pruneda gave on Austin's KUT radio station:

> The family facility where they're being detained, this barbed wire that you see out here is for the safety of those that we have housed inside of the facility. We have to protect them, because English is not their first language. It's their second language. And so we have to make sure that they're secure and they're safe.

Brilliant!! Why hadn't we thought of that? That explains everything.

Of course, if it hadn't been for ICE, the immigrant families now incarcerated in Hutto wouldn't have been there in the first place.

For a while, it was possible to hope that the new administration might mean a change in policies for immigrant detention and immigrant family detention. But, pretty soon, it became clear the political wind was blowing the other way.

Here's what was happening. The United States has an estimated twelve million people living, working, and paying taxes within our borders who don't have documents. What almost no one knows is that not one of these twelve million has what's called "a path to citizenship." There is no way they can become a U.S. citizen except to leave here, go back to their country of origin, and apply for a visa to come back. If they're lucky enough to get the visa—highly unlikely in the case of low-income would-be immigrants—and arrive in the United States, they can then apply to become a citizen.

Furthermore, for most people who want to immigrate to the United States, there's simply no legal way to do so. Even those who are fleeing conflict and violence have no real mechanism for documented immigration.

Today, my maternal grandmother Rae Sterling Aronson, who fled Poland in the 1890s after horseback-mounted Cossacks rampaged through her community in a state-sponsored pogrom, would almost certainly have had no legal way to come to this country and safety.

The current situation is as unfair as it's unrealistic. Though many immigrants came to the United States because they were economically unable to care for their families, others fled their home countries because they were at risk of torture and execution. They were not immigrants, but political refugees seeking asylum. To send them back would in many cases be a virtual death sentence.

In fact, many of the parents imprisoned with Denia at Hutto requested asylum at the border crossing. They were never in this country without papers, since they began a legal asylum process immediately—but they were still detained.

The right wing, ignoring all practical and humanitarian concerns, had a simple answer: Get rid of every single immigrant who doesn't have documents. The truth, though, is that there's no way the United States is going to send twelve million people "back where they came from"—although in 2007 the Department of Homeland Security published an official report in which they planned doing exactly that.

Still, while right-wing candidates, elected officials, and talk radio hosts may rant about deporting every undocumented immigrant, even they know it's not going to happen. It's just a convenient way to play the race card that got stuck back in the deck when African Americans developed serious voting power— as those who are now undocumented immigrants will do not long from now.

Furthermore, it's not as if these twelve million U.S. residents, some of whom had been in the country for decades, had arrived uninvited. As Frank Sharry, founder of America's Voice, a national organization that works to realize the promise of workable and humane comprehensive immigration reform, often says, "We've got a 'Do Not Enter' sign at the border, and a 'Help Wanted' sign a hundred yards in."

If the right-wingers thought they had a solution, corporate America was under no such illusions. The great majority of the twelve million undocumented immigrants who were not children were hard workers. Deport them all, and whole U.S. industries would collapse for lack of employees, from agribusiness and construction to hotels and restaurants.

So there were many reasons for the Obama administration to push for federal legislation that made citizenship a real option for as many of the twelve million as possible. It was not only the right thing to do, it would be a solid investment in the Democratic Party's future. Millions of freed slaves and their descendants had never forgotten that it was Republican president Abraham Lincoln who signed the Emancipation Proclamation. As a result, African Americans had voted Republican for generations, switching allegiance to the Democrats only during President Franklin Delano Roosevelt's New Deal. The leaders of the Democratic Party hoped and expected that the newly minted citizens would have similarly long memories and, as my bluegrass buddies would say, remember to "dance with them what brung them."

But pro-citizenship Democrats from President Obama on down also knew how hard they were going to be hit for taking that stance. True, there were ready, common-sense, workable solutions available. Still, for their party's long-term self-interest, they needed to protect their flanks, particularly from the attacks they knew would come from the right.

The new administration had another option, which presented a potentially serious danger to efforts, not just to close Hutto, but to end all immigrant detention. They could trade legalization for more detention and border enforcement, coming down even harder on some immigrants, attempting to create a deterrent by making an example of them, hitting them with the full force of the law. If the new administration chose to expand rather than abolish immigrant family detention, it could lay claim to being both "tough on crime" (regardless of the fact that the detainees were not in any sense criminals) and "tough on illegal immigrants."

Whether this would in any way protect their vulnerable flanks against conservative attacks, or make a path to citizenship more politically realistic, was another question. But the option to make immigrant family detention even more extreme than it had been was definitely there. For Grassroots Leadership, there was clearly no time to lose, if we were really going to get the families out of Hutto.

Given the alignment of forces nationally, and the high stakes involved politically and economically, most reasonable people would have said, "That's impossible. You'll never get those kids out of there."

But we're not "reasonable people." We're organizers. We expect the impossible—and we know how to do our work in situations that others see as hopeless. One way or another, Grassroots Leadership and our local, state, and national allies were going to get those kids and their parents out of Hutto.

Know When to Raise the Stakes

In the city of Warsaw, such a long time ago
Two hundred children stand lined row on row
With their freshly washed faces
And freshly washed clothes
The children of Poland, who never grow old

In the orphanage yard not a child remains
The soldiers have herded them down to the trains
Carry small flasks of water and bags of dry bread
To march in the ranks of the unquiet dead

With their small Jewish faces and pale haunted eyes
They march hand in hand down the street
No one cries, no one laughs
No one looks, no one turns, no one talks
As they walk down the streets
Where my grandparents walked

Had my grandparents stayed in that dark bloody land
My own children too
Would have marched hand in hand
To the beat of the soldiers, the jackbooted stamp
That would measure their lives
'Til they died in those camps

The cries of my children at night take me back
To those pale hollow faces in stark white and black
Only the blood of the children remains
It runs in the streets—and it runs in our veins

*I*t has to be said that I took the incarceration of children and families at Hutto very personally. Growing up, I spent hours staring at the Nazi propaganda photographs my uncle Charlie Aronson, my mother's younger brother, had found during his Army service in Europe in World War II and given to me. I was mesmerized and shaken by images of grinning Nazi soldiers rounding up terrified Jewish families and marching them, hands stretched high in the air, six-pointed yellow stars on their sleeves, to destinations from which almost none of them would ever return. I sat with Mom and Pop looking through old family photo albums, dramatic in black and white.

"Who's that?" I asked, pointing to the photo of a handsome woman in a long black dress.

"That's your great-grandmother."

"What happened to her?"

"We don't know. The letters stopped coming in 1943."

But when the film *Hutto: America's Family Prison* refers to "the largest trend of family internment since World War II," it isn't talking about what the Nazis did in Europe. The reference is to what we did right here in the United States. President Ronald Reagan, in his remarks just before signing the Civil Liberties Act of 1988, said it exactly like it was:

We gather here today to right a grave wrong. . . . More than forty years ago . . . 120,000 persons of Japanese ancestry living in the United States were forcibly removed from their homes and placed in makeshift internment camps. This action was taken without trial, without jury. It was based solely on race.

Based solely on race? Well, yes, you might say that. In fact, to a remarkable extent, the debate in the United States around immigration has always really been about race. Just as the raw racism against African Americans had helped justify putting hundreds of thousands into the convict lease system and onto chain gangs; just as Japanese Americans had been demonized in the early 1940s so that the public would support moving over one hundred thousand human beings into what were in effect American concentration camps; so now self-interested voices were stirring up fear of and hatred against immigrants. They may not have said the words, but everyone knew about whom they were talking. As I wrote in a review of Mark Dow's excellent book *American Gulag*, in the journal *New Politics*, about immigrant detention in the United States and the role of the INS (Immigration and Naturalization Service), forerunner to today's ICE:

> Prisons, after all, are about many things, and different things at different times. But in the U.S., they are always about race. The INS, in the current Home Sweet Homeland Security era, is not just detaining immigrants. It is very specifically detaining immigrants of color. New York reportedly has over a hundred thousand undocumented immigrants from Ireland alone, but you don't see INS agents raiding the St. Patrick's Day parade.

~~~

By early 2008, the campaign to close Hutto was going well, building momentum. If we could shut Hutto, we could then shift our attention to the much smaller immigrant family detention center in Berks County, Pennsylvania, just a little distance from Philadelphia. If we could close both Hutto and Berks County, that would mean at least a temporary end to immigrant family detention, the closing of a sordid chapter in this country's history.

Then, on May 18, 2008, the *Los Angeles Times* reported that ICE had issued a "pre-solicitation notice" that stated in part:

> This pre-solicitation is for the procurement of up to three (3) non-criminal family residential facilities with the capacity to house a maximum population of 200 residents each using minimal security for juveniles and their families in a safe and secure environment while in the custody of the Immigration & Customs Enforcement (ICE). It is expected families may be comprised of a ratio of up to three (3) juveniles to every one (1) adult.

We were stunned. Translated into everyday language, the notice meant that ICE was planning to expand, not eliminate, the practice of immigrant family detention.

Now we weren't just talking about Texas and Pennsylvania. If ICE succeeded in establishing these three new facilities, filling them with immigrant children and their parents, immigrant family detention would be institutionalized as a permanent part of the U.S. response to immigration. "Family detention centers," by any name, would become the wave of the future, and a lot of people would drown in that wave.

Could Grassroots Leadership organize a national campaign to end immigrant family detention once and for all? Was it time to raise the stakes?

~~~

So how does an organization with a total personnel roster of seven full-time paid staff, two volunteers working half time, and one student research intern take on a national campaign against the combined forces of ICE, the Department of Homeland Security, the Bush administration, and the for-profit private prison industry? And these are only the main players fighting, not only to keep Hutto open, but to expand and institutionalize immigrant family detention, so that even more kids would be growing up in prison.

To paraphrase the Beatles: We get by with a little help from our friends.

But first you need to find out if your friends are willing and able to help—and, if they are, whether all of you working together are really going to be able to get by.

To those who haven't done organizing, the answer would probably seem simple. If the issue is critical, you just make the decision to take it on, and then work to develop what you hope will be a winning strategy.

In fact, as experienced organizers know, the answer is exactly the opposite. First you put together the most promising potential strategies and tactics you can imagine, developing as many alternatives as you can. Then you evaluate each possible approach to the issue, your organizational skills and capacities, the nature and reliability of your potential allies. Only when it's clear there is a strategy that makes sense and has a realistic shot at winning do you decide to take on the campaign.

Through the summer and fall of 2008, that's what we did. Working with Grassroots Leadership's then volunteer communications coordinator Carol Sawyer, now a member of the staff, we developed potential arguments and talking points aimed at different constituencies. Emails carried hard questions back and forth. Who has the authority to close these facilities? Were we better off trying to get a presidential executive order, or working to get federal legislation passed? If supporters were going to make only one phone call, send one email, write one letter, what should it say? To whom should it go? If we decided to take on a national campaign, what name for the campaign would appeal to the broadest range of potential supporters? What alternatives to family detention would make sense to people who had only a passing knowledge of the issue?

As Luissana, Bob, and I traveled the country, separately and together, we continued to explore options and allies. In New York, the three of us pulled together a meeting with some of the organizations we hoped would play a role in a national campaign. Bob and Luissana presented our thinking, the strategies and tactics we thought might prove effective. We listened as the activists present gave us feedback, critique, and new ideas to consider. We met with some of our closest long-term allies and partners, cutting-edge organizations such as the Detention Watch Network, whose involvement would be key to any campaign we tried to launch.

Slowly a consensus emerged: Not only was it critical that Grassroots Leadership organize a national Campaign to End Immigrant Family Detention (by now we had agreed to use that name if we decided to move forward), we actually had the ability, the capacity, the partners and allies to do it.

We could afford to raise the stakes.

~~~

For almost thirty years, the Grassroots Leadership board of directors has held its annual meeting the weekend after Election Day. Some years, looking at the results, we just do our best to keep each other from sinking into depression. Other years are mixed: a victory here, a defeat there.

The gathering in November 2008 was celebratory and hopeful. Not only had Barack Obama been elected, many progressives around the country had won their races. In South Carolina, the winners included former Grassroots Leadership board co-chair Anton Gunn, an African American elected to the state House of Representatives in a majority-white district, and former staff member Kamau Marcharia, reelected to the Fairfield County Commission.

In formal meetings, in the hallways, over drinks, in different combinations, we talked. Yes, we agreed, a national Campaign to End Immigrant Family Detention made sense. It was the right thing to do. There was a thoughtful plan we believed we could carry out. Our long-term allies were with us. There was no assurance of victory, but, as I've said earlier, if you don't fight, you lose every time.

When the board meeting was over, Luissana, Bob, and I drove up into the North Carolina mountains. In a cabin just below the Blue Ridge Parkway, over moonshine and wine, we fine-tuned plans for the campaign. When we came down, we were as ready as we'd ever be.

~~~

It was Bob Libal's idea to launch the Campaign to End Immigrant Family Detention the day after inauguration day. President Obama would have his first hundred days. We would have ours.

Via email blasts, Facebook, and phone calls, the call went out to our friends and allies, asking them to be part of what we were now calling "100 Days, 100 Actions." To kick off the series of events, organizers from Austin and San Antonio held a vigil at the San Antonio ICE office. Over the course of the hundred days, groups around the country gathered to watch *Hutto: America's Family Prison*; held parties at which everyone wrote to the new administration, asking for an end to immigrant family detention; and organized vigils in front of the T. Don Hutto facility and at ICE offices. Via Facebook, we launched a petition drive, asking people to add their names to a statement addressed to President Barack Obama and Secretary of Homeland Security Janet Napolitano:

> Immigrant children and their families should not
> be held behind bars. Immigration and Customs
> Enforcement (ICE) incarcerates entire families while
> they await immigration hearings, often for months
> on end. Corrections Corporation of America operates
> the infamous T. Don Hutto family detention center in
> Taylor, Texas for profit.

> There are alternatives to family detention that keep
> families together and out of jail. ICE should release
> families on personal recognizance, use reasonable
> personal bonds, and provide limited supervised release
> programs.

> Instead of implementing these programs, ICE has
> proposed the construction of three new family
> detention centers. We, the undersigned, call for the
> immediate closing of the T. Don Hutto detention center
> and an end to family detention.

Within a month, over fifty thousand people had signed the petition. The signers came not only from the United States, but also from dozens of countries around the world. Clearly, the word was beginning to get out. People were not only listening, they were taking action.

That was the whole point. To launch the Campaign to End Immigrant Family Detention successfully, we had to get the word out much more broadly than we had before. Film screenings and letter-writing parties may involve a couple dozen people at a time, and are critical to any campaign. But they don't in and of themselves create enough momentum and visibility to begin to influence national policy.

Unlike the for-profit private prison corporations, small non-profit organizations such as Grassroots Leadership don't have the financial resources to hire media consultants and purchase paid advertising. So we turn to what's called "free media," organizing events that the media will want, or have to, cover. For all media, these events need to be dramatic; for TV, they need to be visual as well.

One highly visual event was the annual pre-Christmas vigil at Hutto. On Saturday, December 20, 2008—even before the official launch of the campaign—organizers delivered more than five hundred toys, books, and children's clothes to the facility. Unable to gain entrance to the detention center, they piled their gifts onto tables in front of the facility. Eventually, some Hutto employees came out, gathered the packages, and took them inside to give to the children who couldn't get out—but not before the cameras had rolled, bringing the images of detention and toys to a broader audience.

Then there was Valentines Day. Over the Internet, we sent out the word:

About 130 children will be incarcerated on Valentines Day. The warden at the T. Don Hutto family detention center won't tell us their names, but the children at Hutto need to know we're thinking of them. *Send them Valentines!*

Of course, you don't want to send a Valentine designed for a four-year-old to a seventeen-year-old. So, just below our message, we included a heartbreaking list with the ages of the littlest Hutto prisoners:

5—infants

5—one-year-olds

10—two- and three-year-olds

15—four- and five-year olds

15—six- and seven-year-olds

15—eight- and nine-year-olds

15—ten- and eleven-year-olds

15—twelve- and thirteen-year-olds

20—fourteen- and fifteen-year-olds

15—sixteen- and seventeen-year-olds

If the warden, in providing us with the ages of the children, had rounded the numbers off a little, it was close enough to the truth. People responded. The Students for a Democratic Society chapter at the University of Houston wrote that they'd sent eighty-five valentines to the detained children as part of their "Love Across Borders" program, and wanted to organize an event at Hutto the next month.

When it came to the media, we also got by with a little help from our friends. The timing of award-winning author Courtney E. Martin's article in *The American Prospect Online* on the second of February couldn't have been better:

> First and foremost, immigrant family detention must stop. On Jan. 21, Grassroots Leadership . . . launched a campaign with this goal, calling it 100 Actions in 100 Days. Given the new administration, hope for immigration reform, and a renewed focus on addressing corporate corruption, it's an opportune time to reactivate the country around this issue.

In March, at the South by Southwest film festival in Austin, we organized around the release of *The Least of These*, a documentary featuring the stories of many of the families detained at Hutto. The film sparked another wave of national media scrutinizing the prison.

The word was certainly getting out, not just in the United States but internationally. TV crews from Japan and France came to Hutto. So did the entire Grassroots Leadership board and staff, watching from across the road while Matthew Gossage filmed me standing in front of the giant immigrant family detention center, singing my new song *Hutto*, so we could get it up on our website.

We were definitely getting by with a little help from our friends. As it happens, many of my personal friends are musicians, poets, storytellers, actors, and assorted other artists. When you're a creative community organizer, you go not only with what you know, but with whom you know.

We live in the Internet age, but personal relationships still count, especially when you're asking people to do something. We wanted artists to become active in the campaign. So we decided to organize a new group, Artists United to End Immigrant Family Detention. To help launch Artists United, Carol Sawyer created an e-toolkit for the Grassroots Leadership website. The e-toolkit included everything any artist would need, including sample text and the campaign logo that they could include in their newsletter or on their website.

Most importantly, it had a list of things they could do. Too often, when we ask a potential volunteer for help on a campaign, the conversation goes like this:

> Organizer: I'm really hoping you'll be able to help us on this campaign.
>
> PV: I'd love to. What can I do?
>
> Organizer: We have so many needs, whatever you do will be great.
>
> PV: I'm glad to help any way I can.
>
> Organizer: That's wonderful! Thank you so much.

In this situation, it's doubtful that the potential volunteer will do anything or that, if they do, it will actually be helpful to the campaign. More effective when recruiting volunteers is to give them a specific list of things the campaign needs and let them choose. For Artists United, the list we put on the Grassroots Leadership website and handed out as we traveled looked like this:

> *Grassroots Leadership* invites artists, musicians, and poets to help spread the word about immigrant family detention. **What YOU can do:**
>
> ▶ Publicly endorse the Campaign to End Immigrant Family Detention
>
> ▶ Make a brief announcement about the Campaign at your concerts and, where appropriate, pass the hat and send contributions to the Campaign
>
> ▶ Write and/or record a song about immigrant family detention

- ▶ Put information about the Campaign to End Immigrant Family Detention on your website and in your newsletters

- ▶ Include a link to Grassroots Leadership on your e-newsletters asking your fans to support the Campaign by joining the Action Team

- ▶ Mention the Campaign when you are interviewed on the radio or in other media

- ▶ Help create a multi-artist CD to be distributed to DJs internationally

- ▶ Include a note about the Campaign on your next CD asking folks to sign up and contribute at the Grassroots Leadership website

- ▶ Distribute or display campaign materials at your merchandise table

- ▶ Include logos, text, and tools from the e-toolkit in your newsletters, website, and other materials

In Memphis in February, we set up a booth at the Folk Alliance conference, the annual gathering of the folk music community. Carol Sawyer and LaWana Mayfield, coordinator of Grassroots Leadership's Mecklenburg Justice Project in Charlotte, North Carolina, worked the booth; I worked the crowd. Over one hundred and forty people joined.

For that occasion and, now that I think of it, from inauguration day on, I never changed T-shirts. Just so you don't worry about my commitment to public health, let me be absolutely clear: I wore different T-shirts, but they were all identical. For a weeklong trip, I'd pack at least three, all of them black with white lettering, that read "End Immigrant Family Detention. No more families behind bars." The letters were literally behind bars themselves. Underneath, in black letters on white, was our website: www.GrassrootsLeadership.org.

It was fun being a walking human billboard. In general, my preferred mode was the T-shirt alone with jeans. It was printed on both front and back, so everyone could see me coming and going. Besides, it was summer. If the temperature dropped, I'd put the shirt over a long-sleeved T-shirt or sweatshirt. For more formal occasions, I'd wear the T-shirt under a sport jacket. Over time, I became expert at holding the lapels back with my elbows, so the entire message could be seen and read.

~~~

I flew to Texas on the first Monday of August 2009. Bob Libal met me at the Austin airport. We drove down César Chávez Boulevard to the Grassroots Leadership office, which we share with our friends and landlords PODER, a vibrant local organization that has worked for years on issues of environmental racism. In the back room that passed for conference space, over endless cups of coffee and a steady stream of breakfast tacos, we spent two days analyzing and debriefing the campaign.

There was good news and bad news. On the one hand, we agreed, our work and that of our allies had helped make Hutto the best-known (and probably worst-liked) immigrant detention center and the most notorious for-profit private prison in the United States. People and organizations all over the country had taken part in our 100 Days, 100 Actions kickoff and were continuing to take actions.

Media, both new and traditional, had been at least as good as we'd expected. Almost seventy thousand people had signed our Facebook petition, and nearly four thousand had joined our "Cause." We were communicating with all of them regularly. Several members of Artists United had written songs about Hutto and were working to support the campaign. Our allies in Washington were working hard to make sure the grassroots organizing message was being heard in the halls of Congress and at the White House.

On the other hand, the Obama administration, which had taken office the day before we launched the campaign, hadn't shown any signs of acting to eliminate immigrant family detention. There were rumors that they might move to improve the appalling conditions in all immigrant detention centers by placing federal monitors in them—from our perspective a move in the wrong direction, making it even harder to shut Hutto down. We still hadn't a clue where ICE planned to put the three new immigrant detention centers, or even whether they'd secretly signed contracts to build them.

It was time to raise the stakes again. The next step, we decided, would be to take the seventy-thousand-name petition to Washington, to try to present it to President Barack Obama and First Lady Michelle Obama. The Detention Watch Network was holding a national meeting in late September, which many of our key allies would be attending. We would ask them all to join us in a major media event, perhaps in front of the White House.

The next day, Wednesday, August 5, Bob, Luissana, and I drove to Houston to interview potential organizers for the new office Grassroots Leadership was opening in that city. The candidates were wonderful. The interviews were exciting as well as informative.

Afterwards, satisfied with a good three days' work, we sat at the round table in the coffeehouse where we'd been holding court since early morning, finally eating lunch and, in deference to the fact that we were after all in Texas, happily drinking longnecks. I was in a great mood, glad to be with such fine coworkers and friends, looking forward to the rest of my time in the state.

I was just drifting off to sleep—a lifetime trait anyone who knows me is more than familiar with—when I heard Bob shout. I woke with a start. He was staring at the screen on his iPhone.

"What's wrong?" I imagined the worst.

"There's about to be a major announcement from the White House. The administration is going to issue a new policy on immigrant detention."

I froze. Was this the moment we'd hoped for—or the moment we'd dreaded? Would they close Hutto, perhaps even end immigrant family detention once and for all? Would they announce that they were going to build three new family detention centers? Were we about to win—or about to lose?

The coffeehouse closed for the day. Being creative community organizers, we decided on the only possible strategic option.

We went to a bar.

We sat there on the stools, side by side, Luissana, Bob, and I. By now, emails and text messages were coming in from all over the country, and the rumors were flying. We were flying, too, with anxiety and hope.

The tension kept building as the hours went by. At about 7:45 P.M. Texas time, I couldn't take it any more. I called Elizabeth Minnich at our home in Charlotte and asked her to stay on the phone with me while we sweated it out.

"Wait! Here it is!" Bob was watching an incoming text message. As he scrolled down, he started to read it to us. I held up my cell phone so Elizabeth could hear.

I couldn't believe it. We had won.

They were going to take every last one of the families out of Hutto. The proposals for three new immigrant family detention centers would be canceled. The news would be in the morning edition of the *New York Times*.

I couldn't sleep that night. I still didn't believe it. Every time I woke up, I'd race to my computer to see if the *Times* story had been posted yet.

Sometime just before dawn on Thursday, August 6, it showed up on my screen.

The government will stop sending families to the T.
Don Hutto Residential Center, a former state prison
near Austin, Texas, that drew an American Civil
Liberties Union lawsuit and scathing news coverage for
putting young children behind razor wire . . .

The decision to stop sending families there—and to set
aside plans for three *new* family detention centers—is
the Obama administration's clearest departure from its
predecessor's immigration enforcement policies.

It was real. Finally, I could sleep.

Is the victory perfect? No. Hutto will still be used to house
immigrant detainees without children. Many of the families that
were taken out of Hutto were deported. Others are awaiting asylum hearings that could result in their deportation. Every child,
woman, and man who spent time at Hutto, and all those who are
in other immigrant detention centers across the United States,
will continue to suffer from the effects of, as the *New York Times*
put it in an editorial on September 20, 2009, " . . . the desperate
reality: the brutal mistreatment; isolation, filth and deprivation;
the shabby or non-existent health care."

There is still much work to be done, particularly in rolling
back immigrant detention and deportation. Thirty-three thousand people are living in detention every day; more than four
hundred thousand are deported every year.

Despite this reality, the importance of the victory at Hutto,
and the withdrawal of the proposal to build three new immigrant
family detention centers, should not be underrated. But it will
only remain so if we keep raising the stakes, so that we continue
moving forward, and make the price of going backwards simply
too high to pay.

Keep the faith

Don't you think it's crazy, this old world and its ways
Who ever thought the 60's
Would be called the "good old days"
But like the Weavers sang to us, "Wasn't that a time?"
When we raised our hands and voices on the line
> And we all sang *Bread and Roses,*
> *Joe Hill,* and *Union Maid*
> We linked our arms and told each other
> "We are not afraid!"
> *Solidarity Forever* would go rolling through the hall
> *We Shall Overcome* together, one and all

The more I study history, the more I seem to find
That in every generation there are times just like that time
When folks like you and me who thought
That we were all alone
Within this wondrous movement found a home
> And they all sang *Bread and Roses,*
> *Joe Hill,* and *Union Maid*
> They linked their arms and told each other
> "We are not afraid!"
> *Solidarity Forever* would go rolling through the hall
> *We Shall Overcome* together, one and all

Though each generation fears that it may be the last
Our presence here is witness to the power of the past
And just as we have drawn our strength
From those who now are gone
Younger hands will take our work and carry on
    And they'll all sing *Bread and Roses,*
    Joe Hill, and *Union Maid*
    They'll link their arms and tell each other
    "We are not afraid!"
    Solidarity Forever will go rolling through the hall
    We Shall Overcome together, one and all
    We Shall Overcome together, one and all

*M*y partner and spouse Elizabeth Minnich once surprised me by asking, "Are you thinking about starting a new organizing campaign?"

I was taken aback. It was true, but I hadn't told Elizabeth or anyone else.

I wasn't ready to confess that easily. I know transparency is in vogue these days, but I really don't like it when someone can see through me that easily, even Elizabeth. Grudgingly, I admitted that, yes, I was indeed getting ready to do exactly that. "How did you figure it out?" I wanted to know.

"It's not all that hard." Her smile lit up her face. "There's a characteristic mode you have when you're getting ready to build a new organization."

"Like what?" I was not particularly enjoying this conversation.

"There's a particular state you go into." She didn't mean North Carolina. "You get up in the middle of the night. You wander around talking to yourself even more than usual. You get very focused—when people say something, you don't even notice they're talking to you. You hum a lot, like you do when you're working on a new song, except in this case you're not writing anything, just humming."

"Really?" My voice rose to a squeak. "I do all that?" It was like being on the old TV series *This Is Your Life*, except that show only covered the good parts.

She nodded. "May I make a suggestion?"

"Sure." At this point, what did I have to lose?

She looked at me fondly. "Just this once," she said, "would you like to talk about what's really bothering you, before you externalize your emotions by building a new organization, and then spend the next five years complaining about all the problems it's causing you?"

I never started the organization.

~~~

Because, you know, Elizabeth is absolutely right. Community organizers don't just start organizations. That's the easy part, the fun part. For those who are emotionally attuned to this kind of work, there's great excitement and energy in the early moments of a new organizing drive, the adrenaline rush of engaging the opposition, the emotional high when your skills and intellect are running in top gear. You can get addicted to it.

But organizers also have to maintain the organizations they help build, doing their part to keep them going, year after year, crisis after crisis, defeat after defeat.

That's where pulling your shift comes in.

I learned a lot not only about pulling my shift, but also about creative community organizing, from my father. Pop was good, not just at the usual things a rabbi does, like keeping the faith (in all senses of the expression), but at understanding and surviving work, life, and culture in major organizations—the stock in trade of people who do the work I do. Much of what I know about how to work with both people and institutions, about how to stick with a job through good times and tough times, comes from him.

Pop probably would have lived to be a hundred years old, if the Parkinson's hadn't gotten him. His father Gabriel Kahn grew up poor in Czarist Russia in the late nineteenth century, hardly a situation synonymous with good nutrition and comprehensive pediatric care. Drafted into the czar's army at the age of twenty for a twenty-five-year term, he deserted as soon as he could, walked across Europe, and bartered passage to North America for work swinging a pick and shovel for the Canadian Pacific Railway. When that job played out, he ended up in Winnipeg working as a hod carrier.

Most people today have never even heard of a hod. The only time I've encountered the word in the last forty years was on a 45-rpm record by Buck Owens and the Buckaroos, *No Milk and Honey in Baltimore.*

In case you have a hard time finding that record: A hod, just so you'll know if it ever comes up again, or if you want to surprise your Scrabble-playing friends between organizing campaigns, is a flat board about two feet square, with a wooden yoke underneath, sort of like you see on oxen teams in films about "the opening of the American West"—by white settlers, of course, not by those Native Americans who had been living there for thousands of years, for whom it had always been wide open, until the settlers came. You put as many courses, or layers, of brick on the hod as you think you can lift, hoist it onto your shoulder, steady it with both hands, then walk up flight after flight of stairs to where the bricklayers are making mortar magic with their trowels. It's poor people's work, the very bottom of the employment food chain.

My grandfather had a good life, but a hard one, with a very rough start. He still lived to the age of ninety-two. Pop, raised poor but at least with something to eat every day, passed on at the age of eighty-seven. I was with him when he died, on the Fourth of July in 2001, just as the fireworks were going off (a flair for the dramatic runs in the family, as you've probably figured out by now). I miss him every day of my life.

For many years, until the Parkinson's finally robbed him of so much of who he had been, Pop and I served together on the board of the Jewish Fund for Justice (now, after a number of mergers, the Jewish Funds for Justice), a national foundation that supports creative community organizing. I think it's only fair to say that he got his board seat the honest way, through nepotism. The Jewish Fund for Justice was one of my personal organizing efforts. When it came time to put a national board together, I needed a rabbi, so I chose the one I knew best: Pop.

I was the national board chair for the organization's first half-dozen years. Once, after a particularly stressful and difficult meeting, Pop and I were walking down the street in Washington, D.C., going to pick up his Pontiac and head home. After a few blocks, he stopped, turned, and gave me a big hug. "You were wonderful! Just amazing!" He hugged me again, half lifting me off the ground in the process.

I was touched. Pop was always wonderfully supportive of me and my work, and unusually physically affectionate for a man of his generation. Still, this was really over the top. The only appropriate response was to stand there glowing. That's what I did.

Pop resumed walking towards the car, talking all the way. "You were unbelievable! There we were, less than an hour away from the end of the meeting, hopelessly deadlocked on a decision we absolutely had to make today.

"You went around the room. You summarized every single person's position in a sentence or two. Then you said, 'Let me see if I can craft something that incorporates everyone's position, and meets everyone needs.' You presented your resolution. It was immediately moved, seconded, and unanimously approved. Brilliant!"

I was genuinely moved.

"Here's the fascinating part," he continued. "The resolution you presented actually had nothing to do with what any of them had said. You basically took what you wanted done and imposed it on everybody else. And not a one of them even noticed."

This time I was the one who stopped walking. I don't know if I was more embarrassed at having been caught acting so undemocratically, or at having been caught at all.

Pop just stood there grinning.

"You know," I said, "I try to do it only when I think there really is no other choice, maybe a dozen times over the years. But this is the first time anybody ever caught me at it. How did you figure it out?"

Pop put his arm around my shoulders and steered me down K Street. "Well," he said, "you must have learned it somewhere."

However proud Pop was of me, and in fact of himself—for teaching me as well as for catching me—this is *not* one of the things organizers should ever do. When I organized the Jewish Fund for Justice starting in the early 1980s, that was very much creative community organizing, a piece of work of which I'm still very proud. When I became the chair of the board of directors, I stepped away from my earlier role as an organizer and into the complementary but very different role of community and organizational leader.

I was raised kosher, so for the most part I know how to keep the dishes, and the roles, separate. But organizers need to understand how different these roles really are. It's quite easy to slide, often without even noticing, from helping organize a community to becoming its leader and spokesperson—even though you're not, when push comes to shove, really a member of that community.

Still, creative community organizers are leaders, although of a different sort from those who lead the communities we organize, and who lead the organizations we help those communities build. We're more like, well, rabbis.

While he was still alive, I used to call Pop every Friday evening with the traditional Jewish wish for a "gut Shabbos," Yiddish for "a good Sabbath," and just to talk. Once, at the end of a long conversation, he said with warmth so great I could feel it over the phone, "Oy, you would have made such a wonderful rabbi!"

Without thinking, I said, "I am a rabbi."

I could hear the shock in Pop's voice. "You're not a rabbi. How can you say such a thing?"

I hadn't meant to say it. It wasn't something I'd ever said before, or even thought about. It had just popped out of my mouth, all on its own.

But, reflecting, I decided that my slip of the tongue was more right than wrong. Like other organizers, there are many ways in which I am a rabbi (you should feel free to substitute your personal choice of religious leader), just without the religion.

To prove my point: My friend Irwin Kula, a wonderful rabbi himself, as well as a serious Deadhead (that's a fanatical Grateful Dead follower, in case you missed the sixties) once, without any prompting on my part, introduced me to a group of Jewish scholars as having "a secular rabbinate."

I still really like that description. Despite a rich religious upbringing, which has stood me in good stead in my life as a creative community organizer—particularly given that almost all my work has been in the Bible Belt—I'm a profoundly secular person. I assume, given my family background, that I had religious faith when I was younger. But, somewhere during the almost a dozen years that my mother suffered so terribly from cancer, it quietly slipped away, never to return. I don't flaunt my lack of traditional faith, but in this radically religious nation, I do try to hold my ground as a nonbeliever.

If someone says to me, as happens from time to time, "You are a very spiritual person," I say, "Thank you." They mean it as a compliment, an expression of gratitude. In my secular religion, you don't throw that back in someone's face.

What I do believe in, what I do have faith in, is people: the power and possibility within them, their strength and generosity, their clarity and capacity for good, their restlessness and resilience. I couldn't have lasted forty-five years as an organizer if I didn't fully, deeply believe that people working together can make the world a better and more just place and that, in the end, the forces of good will prevail.

Creative community organizers need to have a comparably positive set of beliefs, and to communicate them forcefully to the people with whom we work. It's our job to help people have belief, but in themselves; to have faith, but in each other; to believe a better world is possible—but in this world, not just the next, should there turn out to be one after all.

Just like spiritual leaders of many faiths, it's part of our job to help people feel hopeful, even in the face of hardship. We need to be realistic radicals, pragmatic Pollyannas. We shouldn't be, as Nurse Nellie Forbush sings in the musical *South Pacific*, "a cock-eyed optimist," but we should be at least professionally upbeat, however we may personally feel in the moment.

Some people find my optimism affirming. Others find it more than a little irritating and, well, slightly insane, considering current objective conditions on Earth. "How can you be so cheerful," they demand, "when the world is going to hell in a handbasket?"

Here's what I do when someone I'm working with is depressed about the shape of the world, the state of creative community organizing, the possibility of any positive change whatsoever. In these dark conditions, I view it as a moral imperative to try to get them laughing.

I start by saying, "Actually, deep down inside, I'm not cheerful at all."

I pause and wait for them to say something. Usually what they say is some variation of:

"You're not? But you seem so, you know, so, so . . . cheerful."

Sometimes the only way to choose the precise word for the moment is to repeat what the other person just said.

"I'm not. It's all a ruse."

"But your cheerfulness seems so real."

"Right. But you should never forget that I've been a professional performer for almost forty years. 'Cheerful' is one of my most famous roles. I can play it with my eyes shut."

"So what are you really?"

"Deeply cynical."

"You're kidding."

"No. If you want to know what I really think, we've probably wrecked the earth beyond repair. We've corrupted the gene pool, poisoned the oceans, polluted the air. The only reason the human race might be spared a future of miserable mutations is that we'll probably blow ourselves up in a nuclear disaster long before that ever happens."

"Wow, that's really a grim picture."

"Yeah, well, life can be tough." If you can't beat 'em, join 'em.

"So how do you keep going?"

"Well, I may be a cynic, but I'm also a good trade unionist. I believe in a fair division of labor, and in doing your work well, whatever that work is. When the assignments in the Movement got passed out, I drew the task of being unreasonably cheerful in the face of disaster. It's a dirty, rotten job, but I do it to the best of my ability."

Believe it or not, people usually brighten up at that point, and we can move on to a discussion of what they might actually do about some of the things that are bothering them.

This is one of a creative community organizer's major responsibilities: Be cheerful in the face of adversity and, to the extent possible, help others feel that way.

I don't mean to trivialize the suffering, hardship, emotional and physical pain so many people go through. But laughter really is therapeutic, and hope does heal.

Southern writer Flannery O'Connor, quoting from a passage by theologian Pierre Teilhard de Chardin, titled her final collection of stories, *Everything That Rises Must Converge*. That's the faith of the organizer.

As creative community organizers, we should never encourage unrealistic hope, expectations that aren't rooted in deep possibility. But any organizer who no longer honestly believes that people working together can make positive change happen should probably start looking for another job.

I don't mean that organizers should be unrealistically optimistic, or that the only good fights are the winning ones.

But we should keep the faith.

Conclusion:
Pull Your Shift

You and I have worked together almost fifteen years
We sure have had some times along the way
The road sign said, "To Freedom"
But it didn't say how far
So we just walked a little every day
Suddenly we find ourselves a continent apart
Though the work we do is still the same
The true heart of the matter is a matter of the heart
In these changes everything has changed

Next year I will write to you out on the western coast
Though I know we both will be just fine
The dailyness of conversation's what I'll miss the most
For friendship's built an hour at a time
You and I have worked together half our working lives
This partnership the rhythm and the rhyme
Your constancy and friendship
Have helped me to survive
And understand our work in these hard times

It's not for you and me to finish up the job ourselves
Each generation does the work again

But neither are we free to leave it all to someone else
It's not for us to end but to begin
Far beyond our lifetimes, when work and hope converge
When hard times seem a world ago away
The roads that we have worked to build
Will finally meet and merge
'Til freedom is the life we live each day

The woods along the highway are cold and still tonight
High beams cut like razors through the dark
Traveling through this midnight
Am I headed towards the light
Or trapped within the terrors of the heart
There is no word in English
For one who's shared so much
The work, the pain, the laughter and the load
You are my compañera as long as people dream
Of walking hand in hand down Freedom Road

*H*ow to "pull your shift" was something I learned about when I was organizing southern textile mill workers back in the 1970s. Today, you have to drive a long way through the South to find a mill that isn't shuttered and shut, the machinery shipped to some third world country where it isn't illegal to work children sixteen hours a day behind barbed wire and armed guards.

Back then, though, nearly a million people worked in the mills, three-quarters of them in the Carolinas. The work, the mills, the machines never stopped. They ran twenty-four hours a day, fifty-one weeks out of the year. When they did shut down, so that the workers could take the one week's vacation that was all most of them got each year, they did it all at once, over the Fourth of July, whenever that came. It was as if a great silence descended on the South and hung like a giant cloud over the Piedmont, that area of rolling hills and steadily moving rivers where almost all the mills were located.

Then, the next Sunday night, the mill hands who worked the third shift, usually called "graveyard" or "hoot owl," would come back from the mountains or the beach, wherever they and their families had spent their brief break from work, and line up at the mill gate. At midnight, when everyone had clocked in and was standing by their machines ready to go to work, the entire southern textile industry would creak back to life all at once, like some sleeping giant drawing its first deep breath after a long sleep.

Textile workers don't actually make cloth. Rather, they tend the machines that card, draw, spin, spool, and weave an amazing variety of fibers into fabric. A weaver, for example, will tend dozens of looms, watching the shuttles slam back and forth across the warp at speeds up to a hundred miles an hour. When a thread breaks, it's up to the worker to tie up the ends as quickly and neatly as possible in a weaver's knot, so the machine can go back to work. If the machine breaks down beyond the weaver's capacity to fix it, she calls for a loom fixer, then cusses him out for not getting there fast enough (most weavers are women, almost all loom fixers men), and for costing her production pay.

In any textile mill, the machines have priority, even seniority, most of them being far older than the workers who tend them. Lucy Taylor was for years a weaver in J. P. Stevens's Rosemary Mill in Roanoke Rapids, North Carolina, until brown lung broke her down so badly she had to come out on disability. She remembered the time the threads in one of her looms caught fire. Smoke filled the weave room. Unable to breathe because of her developing disease, she headed to the door to get some fresh air, leaving the fire and smoke behind. A supervisor stopped her and ordered her back to work, saying, "If I need to replace that loom, it's going to cost the company $30,000. If I need to replace you, all I need to do is go to the door and whistle."

Assume, then, that you're a weaver, working graveyard. That shift might start at 10:00 P.M., 11:00 P.M., or 12:00 A.M., depending on local custom, almost as if different mill towns ran on different clocks.

In the town where you live and work, the shift change comes at midnight. About an hour before, you leave your house and start walking towards the mill, maybe stopping along the way for a soft drink or a beer, depending on whether the town is dry or wet. As you get closer, you can hear the sound of the river roaring past, now no longer flowing through the turbines that drove the mill's machinery, but once the heart of all that power and pride. The faintly burnt smell of raw cotton being forced through machines at high speeds hangs in the air; once you encounter that distinctive aroma, you never forget it. Cotton dust hangs in the air like morning mist; workers emerging from the mill are covered with dust and lint.

Under the lights of the mill, the shift gathers, hundreds of workers, in a variety of moods and modes: telling jokes, talking trash, taking a last drag on a cigarette before pitching it towards a half-filled ditch, the glow of the still burning tip arcing down towards the water, hissing as it hits the surface and dies.

As midnight comes closer, you join the line of workers now snaking into the mill, past the clock where you punch in, and head towards your looms. You nod to the swing shift weaver. She nods back to you.

Standing close to her, you ask, "How's the job running?"

"Smooth as glass," she might say. "You should have a good night."

Or she might answer, "It's running rough. You're going to have a night of it."

At midnight, the mill whistle blows. The swing shift hand takes a step back, turns, heads for the door, disappears into the night along the river. You take a step forward, into the place where she had been standing, and begin your night's work.

For the next eight hours, your job is to tend those looms, and to pull your shift as well as you can. If you are a conscientious worker, if you care about the person who will come after you, you'll do your best to keep the job running at least as well as it was when the second shift worker stepped back and you stepped forward. Maybe you can even make it run a little better, so that the first shift hand will have an easier time of it than you're having this long night.

Dawn breaks over the river. Light reflects back from the millions of dust particles hanging in the air. You look up, and the first shift hand is standing just behind you.

"How's the job running?" she asks.

At 8:00 A.M., the whistle blows again. She steps forward, you step back, turning towards the morning and home.

The mill never stops running.

Those of us who today are organizers, rabble-rousers, activists, and quiet lovers of justice did not invent this struggle for a more just and humane world. That fight has been going on for thousands and thousands of years. In every one of those generations, there have been people like us, creative radicals and rebels, who believed in and worked for the possibility of justice for all. That struggle may at times have been driven underground. But, like the river of which Vincent Harding so eloquently writes in *There Is a River*, it has never once stopped running.

The *Pirke Avot* is a collection of memorable quotes from ancient rabbis (I think of the book as "Rabbis' Greatest Hits," although the title actually means *Sayings of the Fathers*). There's a saying from Rabbi Tarfon, who lived and taught some two thousand years ago, that I paraphrase as, "It is not your responsibility to finish the work, but neither are you free from the obligation to do your part."

None of us here today will live long enough to see the just world of which we dream finally come to pass. But it will. All we have to do to make that happen is to do our work as well as we can, in a way that makes the job run just a little more smoothly for those who we absolutely believe and know will come after us, who will carry on the work we have done.

If we truly want peace and justice some day, all we have to do is pull our shift.

Creative Community Organizing's Top 20

But the sun's gonna shine in this old mine
Ain't no one can turn us around

1. Most people are motivated primarily by self-interest. As a creative community organizer, you are always trying to figure out people's common self-interest, the glue that binds political organizations and movements.

2. Institutions and people that hold power over others are rarely as united as they first appear. If you can't get a person or institution to support you, you want to do everything in your power to convince them that it's in their best self-interest to stay out of the fight.

3. Start the process of strategy development by imagining that instant just before victory. Then, working backwards, do your best to figure out the steps that will lead to that moment.

4. It is generally useful, as a part of any creative community organizing campaign, to advocate for a positive as well as to oppose a negative.

5. The more complicated a strategy or tactic, the harder it is to carry out, and the less likely that it will be successful. If you want hundreds or thousands of people to participate in a campaign, you need to ask the great majority of them to do one thing, and only one.

6. You need to believe that human beings, no matter how much they may hate each other, can somehow find some common connection. To do that, leave your stereotypes at the door.

7. In real life and in actual campaigns for justice, the people are always partly united, partly divided. It's up to you to reinforce unity and to compensate for the divisions among the people with whom you work.

8. Don't ever let anyone tell you that demonstrations were only effective in the 1960s—that in the twenty-first century, we need to find other, less confrontational ways to make our voices heard.

9. Be absolutely certain that the people you work with truly understand the risks they're taking, the things that could go wrong, the losses they might suffer, before they make the decision to act, individually or together.

10. One of the greatest skills an organizer can have is the ability to frame and ask questions in ways that make people not only want to answer them, but also to think deeply, and in unexpected ways, about what the answers might be.

11. Laughter really is therapeutic, and hope does heal. Be cheerful in the face of adversity, and help others feel that way.

12. The more sure you are of yourself, of your experiences in other communities and campaigns, the more you have

to struggle to avoid the arrogance of thinking you know what's right for other people.

13. When an institution that has a responsibility to everyday people fails to do its job, one option is to build another organization to challenge the first one and force it to do the right thing. The other option is not only to build an alternative organization, but to use it as the base for a campaign to take over the original one.

14. When those who have been without power gain it, there is no guarantee that they will exercise it more democratically than those who have had it before.

15. The power of culture can be an antidote to people's inability to see beyond their "own people" or situation. Culture can transform consciousness and make social change transformative rather than merely instrumental.

16. Organizers are often unjustly accused by those in power of inciting violence. That's a lie, and it needs to be put to rest. It's just a tactic the opposition uses to discredit your organization. To shut down a prison; to drive an exploitative enterprise out of business; to make sure a sexual harasser is fired—that is not violence. It's justice.

17. Go not only with what you know, but with whom you know. Even in the Internet age, personal relationships still count, especially when you're asking people to do something. When recruiting volunteers, give them a specific list of campaign needs from which they can choose.

18. It's quite easy to slide from helping organize a community to becoming its leader and spokesperson—even though you're not really a member of that community.

19. We can never truly predict what human beings working together can accomplish, and therefore we can never compromise with injustice.

20. The beloved community of which Dr. King spoke, rather than something we reach some day in the future, may be something we experience a little bit every day while, as creative community organizers, we walk and work towards it.

RESOURCES

SI KAHN: www.sikahn.com. Si's CDs and books can be ordered from this site, including his earlier books *The Fox in the Henhouse: How Privatization Threatens Democracy* (coauthored with feminist/public philosopher Elizabeth Minnich); *Organizing: A Guide for Grassroots Leaders*; and *How People Get Power*. The website also has a number of Si's original songs available for free downloading, as well as his writing over the years and videos of many of his performances.

REAL PEOPLES MUSIC: www.realpeoplesmusic.com. For Si Kahn bookings, including music and literary festivals, concerts, lectures, workshops, and residencies, as well as information about other progressive musicians and speakers.

GRASSROOTS LEADERSHIP: www.grasssrootsleadership.org. Resources for people and organizations working on privatization, prison, criminal justice and immigration issues, plus a secure way to contribute online to support the work of this progressive nonprofit founded by Si in 1980.

SI KAHN'S MUSIC

Most of the songs whose lyrics appear in *Creative Community Organizing* are available on Si's CDs. Following are descriptions of some of the CDs that are currently available for purchase at www.sikahn.org. They can also be ordered through your local independent music and bookstores. The songs listed in **bold italics** following each album description are included in this book.

COURAGE (Strictly Country SCR 69, 2010): Released concurrently with *Creative Community Organizing*, Si's sixteenth CD *Courage* honors the quiet heroism of everyday people. With production and instrumentation by Jens Krüger, harmony and liner notes by Kathy Mattea. Eight of the sixteen songs on *Courage* appear in this book: ***Custodian, Hutto, Molly Maguire, Peace Will Rise, Playing the Old Songs, Shoulders*** (*for Brian McSheffrey*), ***Stones in the Furrow, Washington Square.***

THANKSGIVING (Strictly Country SCR 63, 2007): Two songs from each of Si's first ten CDs, plus four new songs. *Thanksgiving* was recognized by the Folk-DJ list, which measures international radio airplay, as the #1 CD, #1 song and #1 artist for November 2007. ***I Have Seen Freedom.***

WE'RE STILL HERE (Strictly Country SCR 57, 2004): A tribute to the courage and persistence of working people everywhere. Recorded live in the Netherlands and released in 2004 on Si's sixtieth birthday. ***Mother Jones' Farewell (I Was There).***

IN MY HEART (Strictly Country SCR 33, 1993): Folk artists don't really have "hits" as the music industry understands them. But, if they did, these would be Si's greatest hits. Consumer friendly and politically correct: with twenty-four songs, the lowest unit price per song of any CD! ***Brookside Strike, Children of Poland, What Will I Leave.***

GOOD TIMES AND BEDTIMES (Rounder, 1993): Si is aware that, despite being a long-time union activist, when it comes to his children, he's management. Still, this CD takes the side of the kids when it comes to bedtime.

CARRY IT ON (Flying Fish 70104, 1987): Si joins Pete Seeger and Jane Sapp on twenty-one songs of the civil rights, labor, and women's movements, taken from the book of the same name by Pete and Bob Reiser. The songs you want to pass on to the next generations. A great gift for children, grandchildren and great-grandchildren. ***Solidarity Forever.***

THANKS

As always, to Elizabeth Minnich, whose extraordinary thinking, spirit, and love enrich and inform everything I do.

To our next generations: Gabe Kahn, David Fernandes, Jesse M. Kahn, Anthea Chan, Simon P. Kahn, and beyond.

To my wonderful sister Jenette Kahn, who is always there for me, and who helps me remember.

To the Grassroots Leadership board and staff, present and past, who have made my work and life so rich over these past thirty years, with special thanks to those who put so much time into helping edit this book: Marianna Dorta, Les Schmidt, Bob Libal, Carol Sawyer, Naomi Swinton, and LaWana Mayfield.

For above-the-call editorial, research, and design assistance: Debbie Alicen, Judith Brown, Dave Beckwith, Rebecca Buckwater-Poza, Elisa Cooper, Matthew Gossage, Tom Hanchett, Linda Jupiter, Lauren Martin, Elizabeth Minnich, Steve Piersanti, Pam Rogers (who compiled "Creative Community Organizing's Top 20"), Frappa Stout, and Paul Wright.

The many friends and coworkers who provided critique, feedback, support, and assistance: Scott Ainslie, Janet Bell, Heather Booth, Joanie Bronfman, Melody Byrd, Katy Chevigny, Carmen Agra Deedy, Eleni Delimpaltadaki, Sandra Dunn, Michael Edwards, Steve Eulberg, Cathy Fink, Danny Goldberg, Bev Grant, John Grooms, Anton Gunn, Geraldine Laybourne, Linda Levine, Mara Levine, Steve Mayer, Chandra Talpade Mohanty, Stephen Nathan, Mitty Owens, Marcia Peters, June Rostan, Julie Rowe, Ellen Ryan, John Ruoff, Carol Sawyer, Dan Schatz, Nancy Schimmel, Bob Skloot, Mary Snow, Micah Solomon, Janet Stecher, Norm Stockwell, Neil Tudiver, Deborah Van Kleef, Jill Williams, Tawana Wilson-Allen.

Angela Davis and Jim Hightower for writing the forewords.

Everyone who wrote the wonderful blurbs that helped make me truly glad I wrote this book.

The musical, theatrical, and personal support team who help me keep going: David Glenn Armstrong, Barbara Ballard, Janice Bane, Allen Bromberger, Marsha Brooks, Cathy Fink, Steve Grauberger, Pieter Groenveld, Mimi Huntington, Rienk Janssen, Don "Bogey" Jones, Jens Krüger, Uwe Krüger, Joel Landsberg, Marcy Marxer, Kathy Mattea, John McCutcheon, Darlyne Menscer, Amy Merrill, Mac Pirkle, Janice Soled, Brenda Mountjoy Sorkin, Jon Vezner, and Philip Zanon.

At Berrett-Koehler, an author's dream of a publishing house: Everyone. I started to list them by name, and then realized I was recognizing the entire staff. I have rarely worked with any group of people who balance sheer professionalism and personal support so well.

My wonderful creative support team: Josh Dunson at Real People's Music in Chicago, who represents me internationally for concerts, music and literary festivals, workshops, speaking engagements, and residencies (www.realpeoplesmusic.com; rpmjosh@aol.com).

Chris Wade of ADASTRA Arts and Leisure in Yorkshire, England, who represents me artistically in Europe (www.adastra-music.co.uk; chris.wade@adastra-music.co.uk).

Jesse M. Kahn, for elegant graphic design, photography, and production of my CDs over many years.

Kari Estrin of Kari Estrin Management and Consulting in Nashville, who provides career consulting and creative radio promotion for my CDs (www.kariestrin.com; kari@kariestrin.com).

Gail Leondar-Wright, who does stellar radio promotion for my books (www.glprbooks.com).

Researcher Debbie Alicen, who tracks down the most obscure references with speed and grace (dalicen@sover.net).

Web designer Mary Snow for making my work look good in cyberspace.

By Si Kahn and Elizabeth Minnich

THE FOX IN THE HENHOUSE

How Privatization Threatens Democracy

Forewords by Troy Duster, President, American Sociological Association, and Amy Goodman, Democracy Now

Available from your favorite bookseller or directly from Berrett-Koehler as a book or ebook.

Paperback, 320 pages
ISBN 978-1-57675-337-8
PDF ebook
ISBN 978-1-60509-271-3

Have we learned yet? Markets are not the measure of all things. Privatization—turning public goods into private profit centers—shrinks democracy until we cannot withstand unfettered financial greed. This prescient book explores how necessities such as affordable housing, health care, water, equal education, and a non-mercenary military must be protected if democracy is to prevail. This book is a guide to returning from the brink.

"Kahn and Minnich cut through the rhetoric of privatization. With this book they hope to mobilize citizens to restore and reinvigorate this democracy."

—Troy Duster, Professor of Sociology, New York University and Past President, American Sociological Association

"If you care about your children's education, the quality of the air you breathe and the water you drink, affordable health care or Social Security, you need to read *The Fox in the Henhouse.*"

—Jan Schakowsky, U.S. House of Representatives

"A spirited blueprint for all citizens who care about renewing America's best and most generous traditions."

—Katrina vanden Heuvel, Editor and Publisher, *The Nation*

Dēmos

Dēmos is a non-partisan, public policy, research and advocacy organization founded in 2000. Headquartered in New York City, Dēmos works with advocates and policy-makers around the country in pursuit of four overarching goals:

- a more equitable economy with widely shared prosperity and opportunity;
- a vibrant and inclusive democracy with high levels of voting and civic engagement;
- an empowered public sector that works for the common good;
- and responsible U.S. engagement in an interdependent world.

DEMOS FELLOWS PROGRAM

Dēmos is proud to be part of a progressive movement that is reshaping the way new ideas inform the public and policy debates, operating on a basis of shared responsibility and shared progress. We are working to incubate and execute new and diverse solutions to shared problems, and to offer long-rage goals that can create stability and prosperity for Americans and people around the world. Through the work of the Fellows Program, Dēmos supports scholars and writers whose innovative work influences the public debate about crucial national and global issues. The program offers an intellectual home and public engagement platform for more than 20 fellows from diverse backgrounds: emerging public intellectuals, journalists, distinguished public figures, and academics whose research can be used to inform the policy world.

connect at Demos.org
eUpdates | Research, Commentary & Analysis | Special Initiatives & Events
Ideas & Action Blog | Twitter, Facebook & News Feeds | Multimedia

INDEX

ABOUT THE AUTHOR

Photo: Nancy Pierce

Si Kahn has worked for forty-five years as a civil rights, labor, and community organizer and musician. He began his social justice career in 1965 with SNCC, the student wing of the Southern Civil Rights Movement. During the 1970s, he worked with the United Mine Workers of America on the Brookside Strike in Harlan County, Kentucky, and with the Amalgamated Clothing and Textile Workers Union on the J. P. Stevens campaign. In 1980, he founded Grassroots Leadership, a southern-based national organization that works to abolish for-profit private prisons, jails, and immigrant detention centers, as a step towards establishing a system of justice that is truly just and humane.

Si has previously written two organizing handbooks, *How People Get Power and Organizing: A Guide for Grassroots Leaders*, plus *The Fox in the Henhouse: How Privatization Threatens Democracy*, coauthored with feminist/public philosopher Elizabeth Minnich, his long-time partner and spouse.

A songwriter and performing artist as well as an organizer, Si has released fifteen albums of his original songs, plus a collection of traditional labor, civil rights, and women's songs with Pete Seeger and Jane Sapp. His songs of family, community, work, and freedom have been recorded by hundreds of artists and translated into half a dozen languages, including French, Welsh, Hebrew, Swedish, Drents (a Dutch dialect), and Plattdeutsch (Low German). Si has performed at concerts and festivals in Portugal, the Netherlands, Belgium, Germany, Ireland, Scotland, Wales, England, Northern Ireland, Canada, and the U.S. He is an active member of Local 1000 of the American Federation of Musicians, and is the official poet laureate of the North Carolina AFL-CIO by unanimous vote of the convention in 1986.

Si is also a composer, lyricist, and book writer for musical theater, with productions and readings at the Goodspeed Opera House's Norma Terris Theatre; the Berkeley, Milwaukee and Tennessee Repertory Theatres; the York and Amas Musical Theatre Companies in Manhattan; and The Nora Theatre in Cambridge. His current works include *Some Sweet Day*, based on the history of the Southern Tenant Farmers Union (book by Mac Pirkle and Don Jones); *Silver Spoon*, a romantic musical comedy that finds Upper East Side WASP plutocrats falling in love with Brooklyn-dwelling Jewish Communists (book by Amy Merrill); and *Immigrant*, starring six-time Grammy nominee John McCutcheon as labor agitator, songwriter, and martyr Joe Hill (book by Si Kahn; songs by Joe Hill). Si has recently been commissioned by the Bread and Roses Heritage Committee in Lawrence, Massachusetts to write a musical in honor of the one-hundredth anniversary of that historic "strike of the immigrants," which will take place in 2012.

ABOUT BERRETT-KOEHLER PUBLISHERS

Berrett-Koehler is an independent publisher dedicated to an ambitious mission: Creating a World That Works for All.

We believe that to truly create a better world, action is needed at all levels—individual, organizational, and societal. At the individual level, our publications help people align their lives with their values and with their aspirations for a better world. At the organizational level, our publications promote progressive leadership and management practices, socially responsible approaches to business, and humane and effective organizations. At the societal level, our publications advance social and economic justice, shared prosperity, sustainability, and new solutions to national and global issues.

A major theme of our publications is "Opening Up New Space." They challenge conventional thinking, introduce new ideas, and foster positive change. Their common quest is changing the underlying beliefs, mindsets, and structures that keep generating the same cycles of problems, no matter who our leaders are or what improvement programs we adopt.

We strive to practice what we preach—to operate our publishing company in line with the ideas in our books. At the core of our approach is stewardship, which we define as a deep sense of responsibility to administer the company for the benefit of all of our "stakeholder" groups: authors, customers, employees, investors, service providers, and the communities and environment around us.

We are grateful to the thousands of readers, authors, and other friends of the company who consider themselves to be part of the "BK Community." We hope that you, too, will join us in our mission.

A BK Currents Book

This book is part of our BK Currents series. BK Currents books advance social and economic justice by exploring the critical intersections between business and society. Offering a unique combination of thoughtful analysis and progressive alternatives, BK Currents books promote positive change at the national and global levels. To find out more, visit www.bkcurrents.com.

BE CONNECTED

Visit Our Website
Go to www.bkconnection.com to read exclusive previews and excerpts of new books, find detailed information on all Berrett-Koehler titles and authors, browse subject-area libraries of books, and get special discounts.

Subscribe to Our Free E-Newsletter
Be the first to hear about new publications, special discount offers, exclusive articles, news about bestsellers, and more! Get on the list for our free e-newsletter by going to www.bkconnection.com.

Get Quantity Discounts
Berrett-Koehler books are available at quantity discounts for orders of ten or more copies. Please call us toll-free at (800) 929-2929 or email us at bkp.orders@aidcvt.com.

Host a Reading Group
For tips on how to form and carry on a book reading group in your workplace or community, see our website at www.bkconnection.com.

Join the BK Community
Thousands of readers of our books have become part of the "BK Community" by participating in events featuring our authors, reviewing draft manuscripts of forthcoming books, spreading the word about their favorite books, and supporting our publishing program in other ways. If you would like to join the BK Community, please contact us at bkcommunity@bkpub.com.